THE SECRETS OF 99 SUCCESSFUL WOMEN

2023 EDITION

By Sharon Brown

The Book Chief

Published by The Book Chief Publishing House 2023
Suite 2A, Blackthorn House, St Paul's Square, Birmingham, B3 1RL
www.thebookchief.com

Book Cover Design: Sharon Brown
Editor: Sharon Brown
Typesetting: Nicola Matthews / Sharon Brown
Publishing: Sharon Brown

THE BOOK CHIEF®
IGNITE YOUR WRITING

Table of Contents

Introduction

Society has constructed a concept that success is measured in assets, wealth, riches and material goods, when in fact most people construe success as a healthy and happy family life, time freedom, flexibility, simplicity and many other areas out with financial benefits.

The aim for this book was to go beyond this and find out what success means to women from every background, and across continents, thus giving us a better understanding of what really fulfills us.

There is a mix of successful women business owners, mothers, artists, doctors, coaches, writers, directors and many more who have shared their own interpretation of success in their lives within this book. This ranges from addiction, trauma, business success, mindset changes, chronic pain, illness and every aspect of a 'WIN' in someone's life.

The very concept and implementation of creating this book is a success to the creator and all of the co-authors within. Many of them have not written a chapter in a book before so are becoming Authors for the first time. Others are adding this to their own portfolio of books they've written or co-written. All of them however, can see this project as a huge success from each of their perspectives. Whether that be to have written their chapter, being published, connecting with others, being interviewed on a vlogcast, hosting a vlogcast, being published in a magazine, attending an event, sharing their story at that event, collaborating with those they've met through the book and so much more...

The whole meaning of success is a different journey for everyone and we at The Book Chief, are honoured these ladies have chosen to share theirs through the pages of this book.

Foreword

By Anca Petcu

Invest Money Tree

I am a multi passionate Mumpreneur, money and property mentor, on a mission to help women create a passive income and reach financial freedom. My main passion and mentoring evolved from my own life experiences of being homeless with three children to becoming a property millionaire. My business, Invest Money Tree is thriving and creating jobs for others while transforming derelicts into nice, safe family homes. This is one of my successes!

*****

Go to any bookstore, and you will find many books written on the subject of success. If you are like me, you may have read several of them. While the books are written by successful people, I notice that many of them are not really offering the authors further, deeper connections with experts in their industry nor a chance for further visibility.

I connected with Sharon through this book and have subsequently been invited to be a speaker at her Let's Talk About Business event through her other platform, The Speakers Index.

Sharon (The Book Chief) takes the Authors on a personal and professional journey, ensuring there are plenty of opportunities to connect with each other on every possible level, whether it be through social media, hosting vlogcasts or being interviewed by each other, zoom calls to introduce everyone and subsequently an event to celebrate the book, which can only further enhance their success.

Sharon is a visibility expert and a multi passionate, successful entrepreneur. She thrives on helping people reach new heights of success and seeks to support them with further connections and collaborative books such as this one, which provides the perfect opportunity to widen your network on a much deeper level.

Book publishing, marketing, promoting and taking the publishing journey to new heights is not something many publishing companies do from my observations, but The Book Chief has absolutely proven they can deliver on a very complicated and time consuming project with many participants. This isn't an easy task for anyone.

In the short time I've got to know Sharon and her work ethic, I've found her to be a great teacher, where she patiently and warmly takes you through your visibility journey. All authors in this wonderful, collaborative book have shared their secrets of success in an open, vulnerable and honest way which creates an extremely impactful read.

Dedication

To every little girl who feels she is not worthy

To every little girl who feels she won't have the opportunities to rise

To every little girl who feels she doesn't fit in

To every little girl who tries to dim her light to suit others

To every little girl…..YOU CAN AND YOU WILL FEEL SUCCESS

CHAPTER 1

SURPRISE PR INDUSTRY AWARDS WIN
By Abbi E. Hoxleigh

I left the security of my ten-year career as a Media Officer at a charity in November 2021 to focus on developing my public relations (PR) business. Within a year, I was recognised as a PR professional providing valuable and actionable industry information considered "tactical or strategic."

What created this success?

Despite years of experience and several academic qualifications, I doubted myself when I started the business. Unconsciously, I had created Little PR Rock Marketing to provide myself with autonomy and a level of positivity during some of the most challenging times in my life. I knew I needed to learn more about business, fail fast and adapt quickly to rely on my reputation.

In my early start-up months, I wrote an in-depth business proposal following a meeting with a high-profile potential client who was snowballing with media exposure. My recommendations to that potential client inspired an article published on Prowly, a PR industry website blog. The article was entitled 'Media Overexposure: How to Take Back Control of Your Media Presence.

I remember the swell of anxiety that rose from my feet into my chest when the blog went live. It took me an hour before reading it back. Writing a piece for my industry was a brave move for my reputation. That was back in January 2022.

Ten months later, on November 2nd, I received a surprise email to let me know that I was a finalist with this article on media overexposure in the Media Relations category of the Public Relations Today Most Valuable Post (MVP) Awards 2022. The awards recognise excellence in public relations. The voting was closed on December 13th. Soon after, I discovered that I had won second place. Machine intelligence, social media, readers, and the judges had selected me as the runner-up.

For an idea of the gravity for me, Public Relations Today provides content for over 41,000 readers daily on their website and through their newsletter. This information hub offers auto-curated blogs, webinars, and downloadable resources that react to reader data to provide the most valuable resources bolstered by editorial teams and displayed at the top of the site.

In its second year, the 2022 Public Relations Today MVP Awards recognises outstanding contributions from many websites. The judges in 2022 included Bob Geller, President, Fusion PR; Dara Busch, 5WPR Co-CEO & Leader of Consumer Practice and Matt Caiola, 5WPR Co-CEO and Leader of Corporate & Technology Communications Practice. 5WPR is one of the largest independently owned PR firms in the United States.

Knowing that I am now considered a thought leader globally has shocked me, as I did not nominate myself for this award. As Little PR Rock Marketing, I positioned myself and my clients as go-to experts and thought leaders, which is tough and takes time. I aspire to be the best version of myself. It also keeps me motivated. Receiving the news was a perfect gift over the festive season.

I am so glad that self-doubt didn't stop me from achieving success.

CHAPTER 2

WOMEN IN CONSTRUCTION

By Aimee-Beth Evans

I'm the owner and CEO of Aimee Evans Electrical limited. In 2016 I set a goal. Little did I know that this goal would change my life forever.

Like so many others, I thought, "surely there's more to life than this?" Deep down, I knew there was, that a feeling of freedom was possible, but I couldn't help doubting myself, asking, "Have I got it in me?"

In 2016, I pushed those thoughts - enrolling on a level 2 and 3 Electrical Engineering course funded by the Welsh Government.

I sat at my computer, stunned at the sight of my filled-in application form. Here was my first challenge towards freedom, and I had conquered it.

I started college in 2017, and I found it challenging, but I'd daydream about the possibilities; "Imagine being able to go to your child's party without letting the boss down!" or "Imagine being at sports day rather than looking at the pictures."

It wasn't easy; here I was, a 30-year-old woman entering the construction trade! But I kept at it, and soon I was leaving college with my qualifications in hand.

"WOW!" I thought, "It's now officially possible to start my own company!"

But how?! I needed a website, a van, and marketing support - all costs that kept piling up; I didn't have that kind of money.

A familiar doubtful question began to rear its head, "Have I got it in me?"

Instead of listening, I became SO determined that I would get through the impact of covid, and I applied for agency work as an electrician as soon as possible and got to work! With a good wage of £15 phr looking after my bills and some expenses, I felt on track...for a while.

With the lockdown affecting me so much, I knew I had a long way to go. Time was flying on, and with Christmas racing towards me, I realised that here I was yet another year on, and I still couldn't see my children in their school play; I still didn't have the true freedom I'd envisioned, how could I still have more work to do?! Why wasn't I there yet?!

But slow and steady wins the race. Little by little, the rewards for my hard work started to trickle in.

Soon I was able to pay for my website. Soon I was able to pay for a van. Soon I was able to pay for some marketing and soon enough, the work flew in!

Once word was getting out that a female electrician was running a company, Aimee Evans Electrical, took off! I even had to hire another electrician!

Every job opportunity got bigger and bigger, with calls for more coming faster and faster. I was on a roll.

Instead of scrambling for agency work, agency workers scrambled for work with me!

One day I decided to call a familiar question my way asking, "Have I got it in me?" and for the first time, I answered without hesitation, "Yes! This is only the beginning!"

CHAPTER 3

BREAKING BURNOUT WITH SELF-CARE
By Alicja Son

Join me as I enter the year 2015. I find myself in a fast-paced and demanding world of social care management, where stress and burnout are daily occurrences written on the faces of my colleagues. You don't talk about it, and if you don't do overtime, somehow your contribution seems less valid, as "busy" seems synonymous with success, but is it really?

I felt the weight of exhaustion and unfulfillment. My personal and professional boundaries were at a crossroads, and the stress was taking a toll on my motivation, joy, and work-life balance. The once bright flame in my eyes began to flicker, dimming my confidence and light; I began to doubt my abilities under the weight of stress.

Fortunately, I attended a three-day personal development seminar, which caught my eye whilst flicking through Facebook. I gave myself the time and space to relax, reflect, refocus, and confront my fears and I opened up to strangers about the struggles I faced. This experience proved to be an uncomfortable yet therapeutic turning point in my life. I emerged from the seminar with renewed energy, clearly seeing that continuing to do what I have always done will lead me to more pain and suffering. Change is constant, but does that mean it needs to be filled with suffering?

I got so "busy doing" that I lost the awareness to step out of my comfort zone and embrace my emotions without judgement. I had been using the model of Safe Uncertainty in social work with clients to help them overcome adversities but had failed to apply it to my own life.

You can't move mountains or achieve your dreams if you physically and emotionally lack energy. My mindset and being "busy" was holding me back. I started small by focusing on physical health and nutrition, incorporating nature walks, exercise, mindfulness, and self-care into my daily routine. I worked on my mindset by practicing positive affirmations, visualisation, and reading books on personal growth. I surrounded myself with supportive people and invested in a mentor. These changes soon had a positive impact on all aspects of my life. I want to share my journey so you can develop a growth mindset, as all these steps applied consistently may lead you to success. Now your inner voice may say, I've heard this all before. Let me ask you a question. Have you applied it all before?

Hearing and doing are like a seesaw; I can listen to things, but I will only do them if I understand the important choice and action.

I want to inspire You to take small, consistent steps every day to improve your well-being, welcoming positive energy to change your situation and make it a success story. Health became my first pillar of success; making it a priority is crucial. Mindset is the first step, and I encourage you to bring a conscious awareness about your actions. Success can be measured in many ways, but for me, it's about focusing on the present moment, energy, and well-being. I have persevered, and prioritised self-care and this has led me to relocate, change my job, start my own health-related Facebook group, begin coaching, start a YouTube channel and side hustle, speak on stages, podcasts internationally, do a TEDx talk, become a published author, contribute to health magazines.

Don't just hear, do!

CHAPTER 4

THE JOURNEY TO FINDING ME

By Alison Wombwell

My journey started when I gave birth to my first child; we first started noticing those very early signs; her speech was delayed, she disliked change, and she would constantly walk around on her tiptoes. It wasn't long after this I fell pregnant with my second child, and shortly before she arrived, our eldest was being assessed for autism. Once our second daughter was born, it quickly became apparent that she, too, was autistic. She would only feed when she was asleep; she never wanted to be put down and needed me to move with her constantly; eventually, at eight months old, she stopped babbling, and her social smile disappeared. I was heartbroken.

There is a saying that a person can often feel a sense of grief when their children are diagnosed, and I felt that for a short time. Eventually, both girls were diagnosed with autism. The grief I felt quickly was replaced by strength, determination and acceptance. Little did I know my journey of acceptance was about to begin.

I remember the conversation like it was yesterday, a professional working with my children asking if I thought I might be autistic. We were having a conversation one day about my battles with eating disorders, particularly anorexia, which I was diagnosed with as a teen.

As an adult, binge eating disorder plagued my life. It was a constant battle within my mind; part of it wanted order, control and rules, and the other would seek comfort through impulse eating, triggered by my internal feelings of rejection and invalidation.

Shortly after that conversation, I spoke to my GP, who had no hesitation in referring me for an autism assessment; his words still replay in my head: "why were you not diagnosed earlier." I wanted to go back and give comfort, validation, understanding and support to all the past versions of me, especially as a child.

I went on to receive a diagnosis of Autism and ADHD. I had become a master of masking both conditions.

I wasn't the stereotype, I was a conformer, a people pleaser, and I realised I had had enough of pretending as all I was doing was traumatising and gaslighting myself. I quickly realised how much I had always looked for the next best thing, a new job role, a new course to study, a new house; I don't think I ever felt settled.

I was seeking contentment, balance, and self-validation. I quickly realised this was common for many women, so after my diagnosis, I realised how much I wanted to help others in the same position. That is when Chasing Rainbows was born, my accredited neurodiversity coaching and training organisation. I now help to support individuals and families at different stages of their journey from assessment to post-support. Do I have any regrets? Not one, because I have finally accepted all versions of me.

CHAPTER 5

THE SECONDMENT

By Amanda France

How long had it been since I was there?

The timescale evaded me, and since my return to the UK from the USA, the passage of time had been in events rather than dates; I resumed my education, accepted a job in a brewery, and rose through the ranks to line management. I had then felt that odd stirring, the feeling of "what next?" This was coupled with the risk-averse part of me that craved security.

"You've got your own office, for goodness sake," That restless churning came to the fore. I searched internally, trying to placate the need for security. An opportunity arose for a secondment; I joined the sales team equipped with a company car and a mobile brick with a battery the size of a suitcase. I went to each account on my printout, armed with an A-Z, USP's and ABV's of every brand in our portfolio.

At my first team meeting, it was my turn to update the all-male team of my first two weeks. It was a mixed report: five accounts no longer existed, two more had been firebombed and raised to the ground, and another was in the progress of being firebombed on my visit. I was denied entry to a golf club and had to make an appointment three months in advance to see the chairmen of four social clubs. I had only managed to get into one committee meeting as they thought I was the stripper and even complimented me on dressing so classy; it was a good gimmick, the designer suit and hair up, apparently.

I walked out with no garments removed, but this was not the case for our competitors' brands. I had converted the other pubs and clubs that had let me into our products. There was complete silence around the table, which made my blood pressure pound with greater ferocity in my ears.

The sales director broke the interminable quiet with, "You went to Ferkin Moss Side?" All the men around the table had been given this area to cover at some point in their careers, and none had been, as it was deemed too high risk. My printout had not reflected this fact!

The secondment became a permanent position. I gained hotel chains, nightclubs and football clubs to my account base. I could deliver a professional presentation from board level to sole trader, but I found my greatest assets were my instincts, humility and humour. I would build relationships on trust. I observed arrogant area managers walk up to a crowded bar and bark at the staff, "Go get the decision maker!" I would sit at a table, watching the way of working and the clientele, and when it was quiet at the bar, I would ask, "Are you the owner?" Everyone should be appreciated, bar staff are an essential asset, invariably a gateway to the owner, and I would incentivise them to offer my brands first to their customers.

I treated everyone respectfully, whether they spent thousands or millions of pounds. I remember winning a prestigious national sales competition; even as I was holding my crystal trophy aloft at the glitzy presentation, that familiar restless feeling was present.

I knew another stage of my career was waiting in the wings.

CHAPTER 6

HOMELESS TO FINANCIAL FREEDOM

By Anca Petcu

A few years ago, I was homeless with my three children, escaping from an abusive relationship while going through cervical cancer and buried somewhere under mountains of debt without any idea if I would even be alive in the near months ahead!

Hi, I am Anca, a motivational speaker, multi-passionate eco mumpreneur, money and property mentor from Bucharest, Romania. Bristol in the United Kingdom has been our home for over 13 years.

Helping women earn passive income and achieve Financial Freedom gives me joy. In all brutal honesty, I would have loved to have found a nutter like me when I was going through dreadful times.

If I can do it, YOU DEFINITELY CAN!

After being in emergency accommodation, the council offered us a house in a neighbourhood that my friends were very concerned about. As my Leltz operations slowed, I returned to the Princes Trust organisation asking to be reconsidered for their business mentoring. With their support, I became the first Living Wage employer in Bristol's cleaning industry, and my business, Eco Cleaning Bristol was born.

I serve my customers to an excellent standard; and before long my tiny business thrived and started to create work for others.

Where can you find FREE MONEY?

I started looking for other ways to make money, especially to attract free money. I interpreted for Romanians and referred them to my bank, which would reward them and me financially for bringing in new customers. I purposely change my bank account for money incentives regularly, which I then use to buy holidays for £9 pp. I Collected shop stamps to get the extra few quid.

My excellent standard of work, the fantastic community I was surrounded by, and my now overly handsome Punjabi hubby made my tiny business go from 0 to a multiple 6 figure business in just a few years, helping me buy our house. I started using saving accounts and small investments like an ISA. Appreciation and gratitude have always been my best friends, including making money and growing wealth. I write down ten things I am grateful for from the day, all free money that came my way, including the two pence found on the road. I would constantly seek the knowledge and company of people who are ahead of me financially.

YOU DEFINITELY CAN DO IT!!! From 15k to property millionaire, interested?

A few years later, Covid came, and we were left on one income with barely £15k in savings. We decided to invest in properties. We got ourselves a mentor, went to auction, and semi-accidentally won a derelict in South Wales for 49k, with only 11 days to complete. We had no clue what a legal pack was or where we could find a solicitor. Luckily, the mortgage advisor told us how to get a bridging loan, so as you can imagine, people in our lives have always been a Godsend!

Now it is a beautiful home for a wonderful mother and her two children. Imagine the emotional rollercoaster I went through when my work and determination was putting a roof over other people's heads. Refinancing from a bridging loan to a Buy-To-Let mortgage and with the value we have added by refurbishing it to an excellent standard, we pulled all investment money out! We went back to auction and kept transforming derelicts into homes, with one featuring in Homes Under the Hammer.

KEEP DREAMING and keep going. It will happen!!!

CHAPTER 7

WHEN SUCCESS MEANS MORE THAN NUMBERS
By Angela Roth

Growing up in a family of ten, with two brothers and five sisters, greatly impacted my life, as I'm sure you can imagine. Did we have all the material possessions our friends had? The bicycle for Christmas, the foreign holiday, the latest fashions? Of course not, but we were always loved, valued, and listened to, which meant much more.

When I married Dirk, and we started our own family, I confess to having an idealistic view about how motherhood would show itself – you see, I didn't understand just how much drive and energy my mother had put into raising us, nor how many sacrifices she'd made to ensure that our childhood was a warm and positive one.

Our first son, Andrew, was born in January 1988, followed closely by his sister, Eleanor, in January 1989. I loved them both dearly, just as I loved our third and fourth children, Jacob and Benjamin, born in 1993 and 2000, respectively. We didn't plan our family this way, but that's how it happened and managing the age gaps certainly proved interesting.......

But why am I telling you this?

Well, you see, there were times over the years when I thought I must be the worst mother ever as our children went through their challenges growing up and into adulthood; we found ourselves dealing with bullying at school, insomnia, chronic fatigue, diabetes, and a whole range of other challenges alongside the normal difficulties any child might experience. We also walked through deepest grief as I lost a beloved sister and brother, who were far too young to die. Life was tough, and I confess to struggling with moments of despair and bewilderment.

But one thing I am very proud of is my memories of a mother who always listened to me and made me determined to do the same for my children. Whether I could solve the problem they faced or not, I was adamant that they could tell me about it, even if they knew I may not like a decision they'd made or an action they'd taken. I promised myself and them that I would always love them unconditionally and that they would always know this to be true.

I don't have time to go into what that meant in practice, but suffice it to say that we have stood with them through thick and thin and will continue to do so, no matter what.

So why am I writing about this here? Why not about the businesses I've run or the pivot away from a failing business into the new and exciting membership community I've created?

Because to me, what I am most proud of and grateful for, is that each of our children has a meaningful relationship with me; I am very much part of their lives, just as they are part of mine.

CHAPTER 8

HOW TO PAUSE THE SELF-DESTRUCT BUTTON

By Angie Simmons

Have you ever felt like you lost days to emotional turmoil? Potentially something happened to you that's derailed your life, making you question what's your purpose; why are you here?

We all start in life believing that we can achieve whatever we want. Still, life can get in the way of that, leaving us feeling frazzled, destroying our confidence, and suffering from high levels of stress, anxiety, and depression.

I know this from first-hand experience. Thankfully, I found a way back in March 2014 and never looked back.

In Jan 2014, I was working full-time as a kennel manager and part-time as a dog groomer. I had no time for myself or my only daughter, who was bullied at school and the bottom of her class. I was struggling from the aftermath of the sudden death of my younger brother, my marriage breakdown, and ten years of mental health issues. I was popping antidepressants like smarties and drinking like a fish, anything to quiet the voices of "it's all your fault, you're not good enough and haven't you got over that yet?" Fourteen years on, and I still haven't gotten over the death of my best friend!

In March 2014, I was introduced to a world of personal growth that I didn't know anything about, something that was not taught at school, i.e. self-care, personal development, and entrepreneurship. I was given a CD that put me on an incredible path of self-discovery and recovery. I didn't know who it would enable me to become or what it would allow me to overcome.

That CD is called `making the shift` by Darren Hardy; it mentioned that you could gain a PhD of your choosing just by listening to audio while driving your car; I decided that I would gain a PhD in me. I listened while taking my daughter to school and driving to work and back, a two-hour daily commute. Little did I know that my 9-year-old daughter was also taking in this information.

It gave me the confidence to sack the boss and become self-employed, to start taking control of my life; it also gave my daughter the courage to stop the bullies and the confidence to follow her dream to become an actress.

As I write this chapter for this incredible book, which is January 2023. I am an entrepreneur with several businesses; the main one I'm most passionate about is being a personal development and mental Wellness mentor, helping women improve their mental and emotional well-being. I no longer take the tablets or drink like I fish I'm an author, an award finalist, a qualified coach, and the founder of the Growth Development Foundation. My daughter has been on the West End twice. She left secondary school with three A's and two A stars and is currently doing her A levels, ready to go to drama school.

I don't write to impress you but to impress upon you that if you make time for yourself and make YOU your number one priority, life can change for you. No one can make you a failure; only you can do that.

CHAPTER 9

MOTHERHOOD SUCCESS STORY

By Anim Joyce

Being a mum is a job that has many ups and downs. I have created a work-life balance - while managing the demands of being a full-time mum and, at the same time, raising my child in the best possible way I could. I've worked within three different income benefits departments in the past five years. My ability to manage these roles is thanks to some of the beliefs I set up for myself years ago before becoming a mum. Since childhood, I have believed that discovering your potential and working hard to achieve it is the key to success in any area of life. Most people I have come across always ask how I manage the demands of a full-time job and being a good mum.

I grew up seeing my mum raising my siblings and me single-handedly. As a businesswoman, she worked tirelessly, having sleepless nights, just to ensure that we all achieved and could reach our potential. I have, in turn, applied the same principle in raising my four-year-old to what he is today – being the youngest author in the world at the age of just 4 four feels like a dream. This is a massive achievement for me as a mum and an inspiration to young children.

Like any journey to success, this journey has also had its highs and lows. There have been a lot of challenges along the way. At one moment during this journey, I thought of giving up my job and becoming a stay-at-home mum because of what I was spending on childcare alone. But I paused again and thought about investing in my pension. Most importantly, I realised how childcare contributed to my child's educational, emotional, and social development. - how excited he was to go to nursery each day and how fast he was learning.

When my child was at the age of 15 months, I realised that each time I read a story to my child, he would attempt to write/draw what he has seen from the book on either a board or in a book. This was remarkable but challenging for me as he would immediately tear the page off and stick it on walls and doors. I am very organised, so coping with this was overwhelming; I almost gave up at some points. This was the moment I thought that there must be potential. I promised to support him in the best possible way I could. I encourage him to observe the world around him and his feelings about it. This continuously stimulates his mind. His achievements at an early age stem from discovering his potential and working towards achieving it.

My child has meant the world to me from the very day he was born. I am so incredibly proud of the way he has grown and what he has achieved at a very young age when children are still learning to read, let alone write their own stories. Publishing them is a dream. I genuinely hope he believes in himself as much as I believe in him. I am immensely proud to be his mum.

CHAPTER 10

A CAUSE CLOSE TO MY HEART

By Anna Goodwin

Early in my career, I lived near London, but the success I'm most proud of while living there has little to do with my work. While there, I set up and ran the South East London Cystic Fibrosis group with my ex-husband, Graham.

My nephew, Jack (now 32 years old), has Cystic Fibrosis (CF). I remember vividly the day when he was diagnosed at six months old! The struggles my sister, Mary, had to keep him alive. She ended up knowing more than the doctor about his condition! He found it difficult to breathe and couldn't break down food. Mary bought many different types of food to see what he could process. It was a struggle, but he has kept going with excellent parental care and good support from the hospitals.

Although always donating monthly to CF, I wanted to do more. Having contacted the CF Head Office, I was flabbergasted when I was given an address that was only a ten-minute walk from my house in Bromley, Kent! Obviously meant to be!

As an accountant, I thought I'd be helping them with their finances. However, when I met the Regional Coordinator, Jill, they already had this covered. When asking about fundraising in the South East (SE), I was surprised that there weren't many events. The SE group had stopped running. Then Jill stunned me, asking "Why don't you set the group up?" Graham and I went for it!

It was a steep learning curve but great fun! We raised £50K in three years, putting on loads of events, including quizzes, fancy dress evenings, a 60's night, line dancing, tabletop sales, carol singing, a firework night and supermarket collections.

The group met monthly at our house. I was the Secretary, Graham the Treasurer, and Dominic was our Chairman. We were lucky as he was headmaster of a private school, and many of our events were held there free of charge.

We worked well together and played to our strengths. Some of us are happier in the background - others are more outgoing. Not only were we raising money but also raising awareness of CF, which gave us all an inner glow of achievement and pride. Also, it gave me a group of friends – and it's not easy to make friends in London!

Running the group came naturally because I'm organised and a good planner. Also, I'm always happy to ask for help when I'm out of my depth; there were several occasions when this was the case! I didn't realise it at the time, but being able to lead people helped massively. I enjoy taking on responsibility and encouraging people to step up.

It was incredible to see the resilience of the CF children. They had so much to put up with, but they kept on going and joining in when they felt well enough. Truly, they were inspirational. Being empathetic was important, as the CF parents could only do what they could, as their priority was keeping their children well.

A special time for me - a time that I will always remember with fondness, glad that I could do something concrete to help. Even though it was a challenge, it was good fun and great to know that with the help of the group, we did it!

CHAPTER 11

BREAKING THE BIASES

By Arpinder Bansi

At school, I wanted to study Engineering. I was the first Asian girl to graduate in Civil Engineering in the UK and earn a PhD designing space shuttles. I went against the community, which believed girls should focus on being good housewives. Attending university was frowned upon, and engineering was an unsuitable career choice. I was even told that no one would want to marry me if I was too educated. To follow my heart, I experienced waves of backlash as people criticised my choices. Even my teachers advised I should lower my ambitions to leave school at 16 and find work in a factory.

Nevertheless, I pursued my dreams and married a wonderful guy. I also raised a family while enjoying a successful engineering career where I held senior positions. As I climbed higher in the organisation, conscious and unconscious biases became harder to navigate. Challenges included a lack of open and fair opportunities, unequal pay and exclusions for being different. I would initiate conversations to challenge biased decisions and unconsciously biased behaviours. These conversations were uncomfortable and unwelcome. But silence would keep fuelling unconscious biased behaviours and inequalities. For me, "success" was to excel as an engineer. Others saw my success as smashing the glass ceilings that hold women back. I am now on a mission to empower women to achieve their dreams, pave new paths and show the world what we are capable of without compromising what we value. My recipe for success is as follows:

Find Your True Purpose.

Take time to explore what you are passionate about.

Find what you want to do and why it excites you.

Understand your core values to understand who you are to find your purpose in life. When you lead a life that enables you to fulfil your purpose, you lead a better life that is more meaningful, happy and healthy.

Empower Yourself. Believe in yourself and your cause to prevent limiting beliefs from slowing you down. Believe in yourself to the extent that any self-sabotage voice is silenced. Practice being confident. Empower yourself with a can-do / will-do attitude that doesn't allow you to quit.

Practice Positivity. Have a positive attitude and surround yourself with positive, supportive people. Practice positive affirmations to re-wire your thinking. Nurture new neural pathways to start embedding new attitudes and behaviours. Positivity enables you to be more productive as well as grow your resilience. Write a plan with actions you need to take and then consistently follow your actions through. Articulate meaningful goals from your purpose and steadily work towards them from your action plan. Being brave and doing something new or different can be scary. It can be daunting to keep moving forward when there is a lot of uncertainty about what will happen next, especially when not many people have done what you want to do while walking in your shoes. However, confront the fear and find ways to become fearless. Get comfortable with being uncomfortable so that being brave becomes a habit.

To be successful, step up and embrace what is scary so that it isn't scary anymore. Following your dreams, challenge limiting beliefs fuelled by society and live a successful life without regrets.

CHAPTER 12

CREATING COMPASSIONATE LEADERS OF INFLUENCE
By Dr Arthie Moore-Robberts

The struggle was palpable as I took a deep breath and reigned in my need to react (most violently, I must add) towards the people sitting around the boardroom. The violent images were in my head, actually, but my problem was that everything that happened or I thought of in my head ultimately fell out of my mouth. Oh, the joys of Freedom of Speech was not always welcomed at inopportune times.

Therein lies the story of most of my journey as I traversed the fascinating Business world managed by many self-appointed, ego-driven (en)titled Managers, yet led rarely by visionaries who understood the nuances of Leadership. And this intrigued me deeply!

I finally felt a rush of excitement that I had found my purpose. I knew now why I walked this Earth. To challenge the Leadership of our Country, our companies, our businesses and even the head of our families.

A spark of enlightenment grew into a real story, and I aptly named it "Creating Compassionate Leaders of Influence!" Now that was only the beginning of the journey. As I challenged thinking, perspectives, beliefs and the programming of how people were being led, I began to have realisations of my own.

My own judgemental beliefs needed to be realigned. My prejudices addressed. My behaviour had to change. A massive pill to swallow! One that I began chewing on verrrrrry slowly! See, if I was going to challenge the thinking and beliefs of others, I needed to work on my mindset seriously. And wow! Getting to know me was both fascinating and mind-blowing.

Empathy is the emotional connection we FEEL towards our fellow human beings, yet compassion is the behaviour we SHOW them in our actions that we actually care. I loved it, fell in love with it and began to explore this amazing thought more earnestly.

As I reflected on what was most important that I wanted to showcase, I chose success, growth, mindset, beliefs and actions as the key areas to focus on.

"Never come down to someone else's level; bring them up to yours. However, if you are NOT evolving, WHAT are you bringing them up to?" – Dr Arthie Moore-Robberts

And et voila, I began to see that evolving as a person was the secret to successful women challenging the imbalances in equity, injustices in promotions, thoughtlessness in communication, disrespect in behaviour, and more than that….not being "seen" as an important contributor to this fabulous World. I thought – NO MORE!

No longer will we be overlooked as bystanders and supporters in the background! Wake up, World, the creators of life, nurturers of life, the very embodiment of Compassion – Women are here, right now, embracing their true reality! Here to be seen AND heard. Innovators, Agitators, Magicians, Healers, Believers and Deliverers of Hope. Let our voices sing melodiously, high above the mayhem of history. My passion is storming through policies and upsetting the status quo in the board room because the reality is this, if not now, then when? It all begins with you!

Compassion is the Compass that Leaders will be able to guide their people out of Complacency. THAT is why I walk this Earth!

CHAPTER 13

MY SUCCESS STARTED WITH A VISION

By Beata Stepinska

As a young girl aged 12, I had a vision of being a successful woman, living in a different country with a couple of businesses, a family, a car and a nice house. My parents always gave me a little smile and said, "Of course, darling; let's wait and see".

Fast forward 30 years.

My first business idea evolved when I was working as a property manager in a real estate firm. Speaking to landlords, tenants, and inventory companies, I spotted a gap in the market for a cleaning company that understood the process from all angles.

Getting the business off the ground was a struggle; training staff, purchasing the products and equipment, speaking to potential clients, bookings, signing off jobs, marketing calls, invoicing, and, at the same time, raising my eight-month-old daughter seemed impossible.

Looking back, I think it would have been difficult without the help and support from my partner at the early stages. I felt this awful guilt and had to make many tough choices as a new mother, sacrificing family time, summer holidays, trips to playgrounds, and walks in the park. I was missing out on many things. However, I knew deep down that I had to keep going as this was the start of our financial security.

Seven years later, after the cleaning business was running smoothly, I wanted to build another income stream. I decided to fulfil a long-term dream and start a property business. I had a fair idea of what good rental properties looked like and what the perspective tenants wanted. This was the start of my second business, and I managed to build a successful property portfolio.

All the above are great achievements, but I forgot one crucial detail: you need an exit plan! It doesn't matter if you are a start-up or a well-established business; you must have a strategy. It is so rewarding to see your business grow but don't become too comfortable. You need to keep improving to be better than your competitors, plus your circumstances or the market conditions can change overnight.

Unfortunately, I had to learn the hard way. I didn't have an exit plan for my first business and, as a result, had to let half of it go. It was a difficult decision after years of hard work, sleepless nights and sacrificing my family life.

My learning: Never stop believing in yourself, don't look at failure as if you lost the battle, and get up and go again. Always learn from your mistakes. Build strong relationships. You don't need 150 people in your address book; you need ten that will support you in whatever challenges you face.

Make sure you have a good accountant that understands your business, your long-term goals and your exit plan from the start.

Books are another brilliant way to learn. I wish I had known this earlier. When you read a book, try to study it. Take notes, highlight some lightbulb moments, and see if you can implement them to help your business grow and balance your work/family life.

Building wealth is great but remember your families and close friends are part of your success too!!!

Thank you to my family; Harriet, Elliot & Paul.

CHAPTER 14

ACHIEVING SUCCESS THROUGH BEING

By Beverly Radley

The pressure 'To Do" is so great. Being busy sometimes feels like a badge of honour society wants us to wear. But I am a human BEing, not a human DOing. That's not to say that the things I do are unworthy. They're not. They bring me joy, and the subsequent feeling of happiness is its own success. But what I want to focus on here is that you don't need to push yourself to be busy all the time to achieve success. Learning to slow down, take a breath and just BE using the aspect of FLOW as the goal. That allows aspects to flow to you.

How can I separate my feelings from others' feelings and emotions without me knowing how I feel? We are all connected, and we learn to resonate with the frequencies around us.

Have you ever stepped into a child's curious world? I hadn't realised that my ability to be present with children was linked to my innate strength of curiosity and joy. Children are naturally curious and find joy in the simplest of things. They don't need to be rushed. Their imagination is beautiful, and their creativity and connection are delightful.

I recommend you take the next opportunity to immerse yourself in their world, but suspend all your judgement and send your monkey mind on a vacation while you do it. The experience of just being with a child can connect you back to your inner magic.

You have the power to be present with another in their world – whether that is the make-believe fairyland of a child, the historical past of a person with Alzheimer's or the grief of someone suffering loss. You don't have to have experienced it, but you have the ability in you to hold space and dip your toe into their world. You're not there to fix or change it; but to experience it with them and just BE!

Being with another and being able to be present is the most powerful gift we possess. It seems so simple! But in this day and age of judgement, mobile phones and fast culture, it's a gift that can be easily forgotten or not valued.

The power of holding someone with no judgement and expectation is just amazing to feel and experience – for you and them.

When was the last time you were truly seen for yourself? Seen, heard and held? With no expectation, no judgement? Seen for yourself, not what you wear, where you live or your cultural world? Just simply you. Even the words "I see you" can dive deep into our souls.

Giving myself permission to 'BE' has had the most profound effect on me; it has given me space to choose what resonates with me and what I choose to let go of. It has enabled me to release feelings that were stuck and buried for such a long time as 'busy being busy' allows you to deny all of your feelings, and you don't have time to feel or time to BE. I'm glad I chose to make a change. My life is so much better. And that is why it's my success story.

CHAPTER 15

THE JOURNEY TO BRYN

By Bryn Petersen

April 2019: our home office, three months from 57. A week of health check-ups yielded a firm indication of the disease I was fighting. Yesterday, I told work; today, I hold a termination letter promising a month's salary.

My PC challenged me. I opened a word document. In a daze, I typed: "Through a kaleidoscope of disappointments, shattered dreams and bitter battles, Anna mulled the paltry pickings forming her prospects for the future".

I looked at the words but didn't see them.

I did an internet search on my job description. Last time, there were pages - agencies, job sites, and opportunities. This time, there was barely a page. The discouraging results depicted a declining employment sector. In a 15-minute meeting, my employment prospects, experience and qualifications are defunct. At 57, I've been 'binned'.

I decided I could look and see no future, no prospects, nothing to look forward to. Or, I could 'flip' the negative and do something else, but what? I flipped back to the words on my PC and drafted my first short story outline for over 40 years.

I'd dreamed and drooled over this since college. Everyone told me variations on 'impossible', 'idiotic', 'stupid' or 'a pipe dream'.

Now, there was only my total lack of confidence stopping me. Then it hit me - a pen name! I could project a public persona. It would be a shield for me to build a brand and a body of work.

My first book is out soon. With no 'funds,' I found the cheapest route to publication. My first book will be the first test to help me find my audience and my way through the publishing industry labyrinth.

Today, I know what I'm doing and where I want to go. I have plans and projects I'm working on. My health is wobbly at best. There's still the nightmare of medical appointments. Doctors still prod and mutter medical words I don't understand and can't spell.

I look at what I can do rather than dwelling on things I can't. Life's not perfect, and there'll be wrinkles along the way. My journey has been rocky, but life is whatever you choose to make it.

You can exist through life, or you can live your life. Life's nicer, happier, and more rewarding if you can smile.

I love the creative process, and being a writer is all about creating. It's about observing, noticing, taking what you see and notice and making it into something new, original and exciting.

Once your story has unfolded, you need to work on it and mould it until it takes shape. Then you have to polish it until it shines, sparkles and your pulse is racing.

I love every single part of it, and I know if I ever tire of it, my creativity will be spent, and it will be the moment to call time on my writing. Until then, I relish every day with fresh eyes to meet whatever challenges lay ahead.

CHAPTER 16

UNLOCKING THE WRITER WITHIN

By Carol Anne Cooper

"Mum, how can you say you're dyslexic? You're a teacher; you've got a degree", my daughter exclaimed after I shared how much of what I had read on the Dyslexia Association website resonated with me.

"Yes, but you have no idea of the effort it took. Just because I achieved that and was in top sets at school doesn't mean it was easy", I replied.

Writing was always hard work for me, trying to find the words to express what I felt and saw in my mind's eye. To me, writing was a nightmare, words never seeming to co-operate.

Maths was a different story; I found it easy, experiencing the joy of learning it. Numbers always co-operated; they lived and moved, unlike words that appeared lifeless, dead on the page, their meaning elusive.

At college, my friend and I spent hours deciphering essay titles, journeying through the dictionary, one word to another, until we finally understood it. I hated it.

A chance conversation with an Educational Kinesiologist / Brain Gym® consultant and the subsequent transformation of my daughter's lack of confidence, rebellious attitude, and not wanting to sit any of her exams to confidently sitting and passing them, going on to study another course and achieving merits and distinctions with her work, opened my world to new possibilities.

I embarked on a journey of personal development and discovery, leaving teaching to train in Educational Kinesiology and Touch For Health. Exploring brain/body connections, gaining an awareness and understanding of systems within us that, if not properly integrated or balanced, have a major impact on learning.

An awakening to the power of specific questions eliciting responses deep from within made me more curious. Door upon door opening to new teachings and learnings through various trainings.

Trauma experienced at my birth, apparently a forceps delivery, unlocked through a process, shocked me. I was amazed at how the pain and upset had been locked in my body all that time, unbeknown to me. It was quite a revelation, as was the impact I realised it had on my brain. Another process during my NLP training appeared to release my words, as I found myself stopping saying a phrase I always use to say – it's like they go into this void, never to be seen again!

Words began flowing.

Along my journey, I decided to study an English Language 'A' level, a subject I believed I could not do. It wasn't easy, but I had tools and techniques to support me now, and I passed it – I was delighted.

The turn towards writing came when a voice in my head told me I would write a book! How is that possible? I can't write! Curiosity overtook me - what could I write about? Leading to further adventures and discoveries of how to unlock the writer within, to help others with their writing through healing inner child experiences and transforming limiting beliefs.

I now thoroughly enjoy exploring words, bringing them to life and experiencing the healing that is taking place through writing two books I have on the go. But the joy of becoming a published author crept up on me through partaking in a Collaborative Book Project.

CHAPTER 17

SURVIVING AVIATION REDUNDANCY

By Carol Lawless

I stood proudly in the upper-class cabin of the Boeing 747, my favourite aircraft; I had been working on this aircraft for 21 years. I was an onboard manager for an international airline; I was part of the brand and believed the feeling of love was mutual. My boss is famous for saying, "If you look after your staff, they will look after your customers; it's that simple!"

It was the start of 2020. I was planning to do my yoga teacher training and give people the gift that yoga gave me. As much as I loved flying, I wanted to develop my skills and feed my brain. I am a mother to three young children, and my journey to motherhood wasn't easy. I developed valuable coping strategies that I felt compelled to share.

I planned to become a yoga teacher teaching pregnancy yoga and supporting people preparing for childbirth and parenthood. Providing valuable support for the postnatal period.

As you know, the universe had different plans for us all in 2020. Covid-19 took over the world, and my company asked if I'd be willing to take eight weeks of unpaid leave. Of course, I said yes; I didn't even question it. I loved the brand; it was part of me. Quickly things escalated, and before I knew it, I had been made redundant. It wasn't personal, lots of us lost our jobs; however, we were reassured that we would all get our jobs back; we just needed to be patient.

I decided to crack on with my plan. I studied and qualified as a pregnancy yoga teacher while homeschooling three children. I trained to teach baby massage, then parent and baby yoga. I was once a Nursery Nurse working for children's services, so I was refreshing many of my skills. Looking back, this was a huge challenge; however, I was on a mission.

I began to build my confidence teaching online to the crew community who were isolated at home, pregnant, or with new babies struggling without friendship or support. My classes were so busy each week.

The feedback I received was impressive, so I kept pushing myself to reinvent myself.

Eventually, the world began to open up again, and I launched my classes in person. 'Carol Lawless yoga' was born.

I invested in 200 hours of Yoga teacher training. I was asked to bring my classes to a beautiful studio in Cheshire. My sessions were picking up speed, and people in the community recommended me. Health Visitors, Midwives, and even Doctors came to the classes as new parents. They loved my honesty, support, experience, and fun personality. The feedback and encouragement was particularly elevating.

I began teaching a vinyasa flow class and was invited to teach at a festival. I won a scholarship place on an accredited infant feeding course. I was even approached to teach Puppy yoga, and things finally started to feel like fun.

The airline opened up again; they needed staff; however, they decided to interview us before employing us again. There wasn't a criterion; the shock was immense. How could that be fair?

Thankfully, I'd built my own brand and developed a product. From now on, I had my very own customers to care for. Survival situation complete.

CHAPTER 18

SUCCESS IS AN INSIDE JOB

By Carole Pyke

I returned to the room and stood by the door, surveying my surroundings. I was so engrossed in the excitement that I had no idea where I had left my brand-new sparkly handbag.

The mix of music and chatter from guests, still seated at tables dotted around the room, was captivating. Adrenalin was rushing through my veins, and my heart had created a new rhythm.

What happened next was unexpected, and I had no idea it would turn into a defining moment. I will be forever grateful that the official photographer captured it, so it is more than just a memory.

Although I was aware of what was happening, I was oblivious to the people moving around me. Imagine my surprise when I looked up and saw a woman walking purposefully in my direction, beaming from ear to ear. The smile was so warm that I expected the person behind me to rush to greet her.

It was only when she put her arms around me and brought me in for the warmest embrace I have ever had, from a complete stranger, that the penny dropped, but I still didn't know who she was.

The affectionate stranger was a British actress and screenwriter Dame Emma Thompson. She is regarded as one of the finest actresses of her generation. Still, I don't remember ever seeing any of her films. The only connection I had with Emma was at that moment, and she didn't want to let go.

Now as I look at the picture of that powerful embrace, I also remember the words that accompanied it. Emma said: "You are so inspirational; it is great to see real people win awards".

We were at the Inspiration Awards 2023 at the Landmark Hotel. Earlier that evening, I had won the award for Most Inspirational Woman. I have won awards before, but this seemed extra special.

I had a second stroke in 2019 and live with retrograde amnesia (93% of my memories have been erased). Add facial blindness and cognitive impairment to the mix, and simply getting to the end of every day is an achievement.

I have heard 'Inspirational' used before. In fact, it is the most used adjective to describe me, but this moment forced me to look at myself and see what seemed so obvious to the outside world.

My success is not the award or those affirming words from a stranger. It is a fact that since the stroke, I have risen to any challenge thrown my way with boldness, courage and resilience, armed with only a smile and the determination to support and encourage others.

Fuelled by Faith, I believe that if we are breathing, everything is still possible, and I am walking my talk despite the impairment strokes have left in their wake.

Success is personal, and we need to define it for ourselves. It is so much more than money or the opinion of others. I believe success must be reached internally before it can be experienced externally.

Your success is a story; your story lives on the inside. Tell it well on the outside, and people will pull up a chair to listen.

CHAPTER 19

FROM DISLIKE TO PASSION AND SUCCESS!

By Caroline Kerslake

My career has been varied, with nothing specific and no big ambitions. I always fell into work and enjoyed what I did but never really loved it. Over the years, my self-discovery of health and fitness changed that.

As someone who didn't like much physical activity, PE at school was an absolute "must I", "but I forgot my kit Miss" to feeling inadequate and not good at any sport; why I felt like this, I don't know, self-conscious, unsure of how to use my body, generally not interested in sport – a combination of all.

Over the years, I moved, but only when I had to! I would change how I ate to change how I felt; I would walk but would often take the easy way rather than any extra effort, and then after my children and doing a few local jobs, I decided it was to time to start looking after myself, my nutrition was good my movement was not still!

From walking around the park with the pushchair to joining a new local gym and having a personal trainer – on a one-to-one basis, no embarrassment of not knowing what to do, but being shown how to move my body, explore the reasons why I wanted and needed to move, to falling in love with exercise (admittedly not lunges to start with!).

As I was in the right place at the right time, I began to work for a personal trainer who had expanded their business. I got confident with my own movement, the possibilities with the equipment, the feeling, changes and the sense of achievement the clients and I got.

After training as a Personal trainer and massage therapist, establishing myself and learning as much as possible, it became time to branch out on my own (that's another story!).

My passion was working with women, predominantly those in midlife – the realisation that not one size fits all was so profound working in the gym environment that coming away and focussing on each woman, her story and her journey was what I had to do.

All planned and ready to set up on my own, I did, just as Covid did too!

The classes were booked in the halls, and the one-to-one sessions in my house were cancelled; for a while, I wasn't sure what to do or how this would work; my career had ended before it started!

But with a good network around me, contacts made, and clients who wanted to work out how we could carry on, we did, and my business grew and flourished.

We went onto zoom, worked out at home, practiced self-care and massage techniques, and worked on our pelvic floor and core, all whilst unable to be in person.

The ability to keep the passion alive for movement and the sense of physical and mental well-being during this time has been my most significant success.

From something I disliked as a child until her 30s (now late 40s), getting to know it, use it, experiment with it, understand it and finally delight in the benefits of it in the here and now and for my future.

Being in the right place at the right time ignited a passion and led to business success.

CHAPTER 20

FINDING MY INNER BUTTERFLY

By Carolyn Parker

I entered the world as the unplanned, unexpected daughter of a naive teenage girl.

I was wrapped in a physical blanket and an invisible shroud of shame, which showed itself in my childhood as a belief that I wasn't good enough, no matter what.

As an adoptee and only child, I put all my energy into being the bright, beautiful girl my parents desired. I worked hard academically and in sports and diligently practised the piano to make them proud of me. However, I hadn't reckoned on having stiff competition in the form of my parent's friend's daughter. She outshone me in every category, regularly winning prizes and medals, stories of which my mother would use to encourage me to improve my performance.

The actual effect on me could have been achieved just as well by using the aforementioned silverware to batter me! I felt second-rate and disillusioned. My goal of making her proud slipped further away every time I failed to meet her high expectations.

Despite this, I went to college, became a physiotherapist, married an engineer, a suitable husband in their eyes and gave birth to two beautiful daughters. I even found my birth parents on turning forty, which gave me a sense of identity.

Yet my low self-worth continued to show up in the sense of lostness. I then proceeded to lose my marriage, my sanity (temporarily) and sadly, my connection with both children, a pattern that continued through two abusive relationships until I didn't have a shred of self-esteem left. I was totally washed up on the beach of life.

Five years went by with limited recovery from talking therapies…

Then suddenly it happened!

I was given a John Rohn CD where he talks about self-limiting beliefs and old stories, explaining where they originate and how we can reprogram our beliefs and self-talk with simple affirmations and other tools. This was a completely new approach to life. It made sense. I decided to test it out by applying what I had learnt. I listened to my negative thinking and how I criticised myself. I challenged and changed this harsh inner dialogue, one phrase at a time. I had found the power of personal development.

Several weeks later, I noticed a change. My confidence was growing. More than that, I was actually beginning to like myself! It was then that I knew I had finally found a way to turn my life around.

Fast forward to the present. My self-belief is such that I've dared to face and work through my past trauma. I've forgiven many, including myself and made peace with my inner child. I believe this golden nugget of self-discovery needs to be shared. The question is how? While pondering that question, a surprise opportunity popped up to write about a life event. I embraced this vulnerability of telling my story, taking it further by proudly completing my first memoir in 2022, shifting my shame and giving encouragement and hope to those who still inwardly beat themselves up.

My secret of success has been the metamorphosis from unwanted and never good enough to standing tall, arms raised, shouting, "This Is Me"

Now my inner butterfly is flying!

CHAPTER 21

THE ART OF FORGIVENESS

By Christine Wright

HAVE YOU EVER THOUGHT, "HOW CAN ANYONE FORGIVE THEM FOR THAT?"

Let me tell you, I held onto this belief for over 30 Years.

It kept me trapped, held hostage, and paralysed me emotionally, particularly around the anniversary of my body being violated, which depleted every inch of my self-worth on Boxing Day in 1987.

So, you can just imagine how many Christmas celebrations were robbed from me in my lifetime. Far too many, for sure. Yes, I was the party girl, a binge drinker, and I drank to help overcome my parents' volatile divorce. Which I blamed myself for at the young age of 14 years. Hence, being excessive with the booze, I couldn't determine when enough was enough, so I used alcohol as a crutch to numb pains and seek the escapism I so desperately needed.

This violation wasn't reported until 2020, as I felt nobody would believe me or see any value in what I was saying back then. I was ashamed and thought I had brought this on myself as I was a drunk, allowing it to happen, as I gave up on the fight. My fight or flight response had got up and gone!

Why didn't I carry on fighting? Why didn't I shout louder? Why did I surrender? Was it really rape if I was drunk?

These questions were all answered, along with many more, once I sought therapy in my 40s; after a moment of divine intervention, that being so, I gave myself permission to become sober and do a lot of forgiving.

HOW?

I started with myself; my first obstacle was understanding that it wasn't my fault and that no person deserves such a heinous crime.

As an adult, I had to connect with my inner child and let her know she was safe, seen, heard and validated. The blame she put upon herself for all that had happened was self-deception, meaning her coping mechanism of choice, which put her in danger, was her way of dealing with it the best she could at that moment. For that reason, I forgave her.

She needed nurturing and to be guided to trust again; the easiest way to do this was through constant daily habits of reassurance through journaling, daily mantras and voice vibration sounding.

Doing this enabled me to reflect on why "HE" did what he did. What was it in his world which was off-kilt? Who were his role models/father figure, and why did they fail him?

In my mind, he became the victim, and I became the warrior. This helped free me from his control. I became empathetic towards him; however, it doesn't mean that I forgot or excused the harm done to me; I just intentionally decided to let go of any resentment and anger.

Consequently, I found my true self, forging healthier relationships in love and life and improving my mental health and well-being.

I now stand in my power to socially educate women and teenage girls authentically about the dangers of having little or no self-worth, coaching and empowering them around the 'grey area of drinking', allowing them to live the life they truly deserve.

CHAPTER 22

HOW SELF-LOVE SAVED ME

By Colette Malcolm

Self-love is the most underrated type of love, but in my opinion, it's the most important. Do you want to know why I feel so strongly? That's easy; self-love saved my life.

In 2015 I separated from my husband and ended up essentially homeless. A few weeks after that, I lost my job and struggled to keep things together. I spiralled into a deep depression, self-harming, drinking too much and contemplated not being here anymore. You might have heard some people describe depression as the black dog; well, I swear I once saw the shadow of exactly that on my wall!

I reached out to the doctors, was given anti-depressants, and was on a waiting list for counselling. I eventually ended up having six sessions, and whilst they were helpful, more work still needed to be done! The depression had eased, but the anxiety was still there. I just didn't feel like myself anymore. A stark contrast to the bubbly, confident woman I was before!

Not long after my counselling finished, I saw a post from a holistic coach looking for people to work with her, and I thought, why not. On the third week, a fire was lit in my belly. She helped me understand the importance of putting myself first and practicing self-love, something I hadn't really done before, as I'm sure, like a lot of you, I was forever putting other people first.

Firstly, she asked me to make a 'self-love' list by writing down all the things I liked doing that made me happy. It didn't need to be expensive nail bar trips or spa days, although that would be nice; they just had to be for me! Then the idea was to do at least one thing off this list every day. My list included running, cooking healthy meals, meditating, putting on makeup, walking in nature, etc. Simple things, really, but these were the things that made me happy. Next, we discussed setting boundaries with people. So not take on all the things I didn't want to do and say no when I needed to.

It felt somewhat alien at first, but the more I did it, the easier it got, and I can honestly say it's like second nature now. I have firm boundaries in place with people and my with my time. I have a solid morning routine to ensure I get off to the best start, and I make sure I listen to what my body needs. Be that rest, exercise, food, peace and quiet etc.

When someone said self-love to me before, I'll be honest, I thought it all sounded a bit vain, and now I know how wrong I was. It has really transformed my mindset, and I'm honestly the happiest I have ever been. I had someone say to me recently how much I have changed, and I know I have, for the better. I fully appreciate the importance of self-love now, so much so that I now help other women up their self-love game and start feeling like themselves again.

So, the next time you aren't feeling yourself, make sure to do something you love, and that's just for you.

Remember, self-care isn't selfish. It's a necessity!

CHAPTER 23

JOURNEY TO WELLNESS WITH CREATIVITY

By Debbie Crouch

As a child, I knew something incredible was waiting to blossom deep within my soul. This magic revealed itself in my 40s. I coped by drawing and writing adventure stories but hid my talent for fear of judgement. Abandoning my creative dreams as an adult, my lack of self-confidence blurred my ability to see what made me happy. Life became a cycle of pleasing others and putting my needs in a box.

For too long, I was too shy to voice my truth, afraid to speak up. Eventually, I experienced burnout and found healing in learning to love myself.

Even in the most challenging times, my inner spirit was willing to create a better life. Divorced and a lonely single mum, I found my soulmate and took my first huge leap of faith by moving away from my comfort zone. Ivan brought out the best in me by encouraging me to become the person I was destined to be. His love and faith reached my inner strength and ignited something.

A second entanglement with burnout left me disillusioned with life and work, and I was diagnosed with mental health issues.

Attending Leeds Recovery College, I met Naetha, an inspirational recovery coach and in her I'd found a friend and mentor.

In 2019 I chose a learn to draw and paint for adults course to support my well-being, where I discovered my desire to share my lived experience and a creative passion for drawing with others.

I used this new knowledge to set up an online group offering a safe space for sharing artwork, positive affirmations and fun posts. I built a friendly and engaged community of over 10,000 in only six months by encouraging members to show their work.

Members feedback:

"I joined because your posts were a ray of sunshine in lockdown amidst all the doom and gloom."

"I Love art, and I was looking for groups where I can get inspired."

"I am an isolator, so it's helping my mental health to do something creative."

I recognised myself as an introvert and overly sensitive, so I knew it was time to change how I loved myself. Using this motivation, I trained with Naetha to be a Creative Recovery Coach.

Eventually, this led me to make a life-changing decision to start my own business Creative Wellness Journey CIC, in December 2020. *"If you choose to follow your life's purpose, one day you will provide inspiration to the world."*

Now, the people I choose to surround myself with gives me the stability to move forward and achieve my dreams.

My business has now expanded into a community hub website, which shines a spotlight on art as a healing tool for the mind, called: creativewellnessjourney.co.uk. Our offers include tutorials and a members' creative-inspired gallery to showcase artwork that supports mental wellness.

This community is a haven to share stories, the joy of learning, and just having a go even if you don't feel good enough.

I believe that the more you can be your authentic self, the happier and more fulfilled you will feel.

CHAPTER 24

LISTEN TO THE WHISPERS

By Elizabeth Calderara

The brakes didn't work. I wasn't touching the accelerator either, but still, my Volvo picked up speed down the steep hill at rush hour towards the first pedestrian crossing at the roundabout.

Now 60mph, split-second decision: if I take to the first exit towards the next zebra crossing, all the kids use this, I'll kill them. No choice. Crossing behind the 16-wheeler lorry, the driver making a perfect circle with his mouth wide-eyed, no time to swear at me. Going too fast.

Straight into the carpark of the local theatre. Another split-second decision; strange how it's so vivid; despite taking only seconds to unravel, it's not unlike a slow-mo disaster movie. It felt like minutes. No!

Not into the glass doors of the theatre, who would I maim inside? The man by the ticket machine moved away towards his car. No choice. I rammed my car into three parked cars and hit the wall. Not a dent in my hard-core Volvo, just the airbags hissing quietly. Goodness, those things smell. The three other cars were not so lucky.

"You took a ton of force in both your hands and arms', said the policeman who breathalysed me at 8.30am gleefully before the paramedics carted me off.

Surgery on one hand and plaster on both and sent away, 'about six months, I think 'when I asked for a healing time frame. Significantly damaged arms and hands do not look good for a reflexologist with a successful business working with children with complex needs and disabilities.

At least I had time on my hands and arms. What to do?

Only weeks before the accident, I had called my Spiritual Mentor. I'd asked, "I keep finding reasons not to leave my current practice, but it doesn't feel right to stay. I feel uncomfortable; my intuition is grabbing me by both hands, pulling me away. I'm worried people will think I'm mad if I quit to become a full-time Celtic Shamanic Mentor to Western Women. It's just not the right time."

"Well, when would be the right time then?" she replied, "I'm sure the Universe has the plan to show you the way, whatever vehicle you choose, to use your Spiritual gifts and connection to nature, in teaching, in person or by writing".

I ignored my strong internal messages and my Mentor's hint, so I received a fast and furious Universal lesson.

It woke me up.

So I typed with two fingers. I learnt how to use Twitter and Facebook. Wrote my course with ease. I wasn't going to put off my happy life any more.

It's a reminder, first of all, to pay attention and to listen to your heart and gut instinct. Be courageous and take action even when it seems counterintuitive to everyone else but you. Your gut is the more intelligent brain.

It doesn't pray to the Great Goddess Waddle. What'll I do if people laugh at me, what'll I do If I fail, what'll I do if ...I succeed?

The most significant shift for me was in living my life purpose. So when you hear the guiding whispers of intuition, listen. Take action. However crazy they sound. That's when the magic happens.

CHAPTER 25

THE JOURNEY TO FINDING MYSELF

By Elke Wallace

What does success mean to you? Does it involve owning and being able to afford material things? Or is it about achieving milestones in your career or your personal life?

Success means something different to each of us. So many people look outward rather than inward, as in "success is something to show".

I am one of the inward-looking people – I have nothing to "show" my inner success to the outside apart from describing the journey.

I was an anxious child, anxious due to my bad sight and my over protective parents' discouragement to explore – often in the form of "you can't do this" statements – and afraid of my dad's loud outbursts towards one of my brothers, who sadly got into drugs as a teenager and became mentally ill.

Don't get me wrong, my childhood wasn't bad. Still, it involved a lot of being stared at and called names due to my different appearance as an albino, especially outside the close family circles. The outside world could be scary, intimidating, and cruel.

Children and teenagers want to fit in and be accepted. They want to belong, don't they?

I learned to cope by focusing on the good, the positive experiences and good friends, but the uneasiness about how I looked and not understanding who I was kept niggling for many years.

Uneasiness, anxiety, lots of "why me" and "what if" questions.

I wonder if that may sound familiar to you.

My first change for the better happened only from my 40s onwards when I started with all my training in personal development. First, it was counselling skills, CBT course and Mindfulness training. They helped me to be more at ease with and accepting of myself; the "why me" and "what if" questions stopped, and I had major lightbulb moments that helped me understand who I was and how I became who I was at that time.

It sounds a bit dramatic, but it was an achievement to get to that point.

The only snag was that I was still seeking love, happiness, inner peace, and calm outside of myself and other people, as in relationships. That only changed once I got fed up attracting needy, unreliable or dodgy guys or those who only wanted a bit of 'playtime', guys who only accepted me once I proved worthy. I reached that point right before my NLP and Timeline Practitioner training, which rewired my brain and cleared away any remaining anxiety and other negative emotions, self-doubt, etc.

I found my inner happiness; I found my inner peace and contentment. I am complete as the person I am. I don't need anyone to complete me. I know who I am, fully accept and love myself, and stand by who I am.

I am a soul on a journey in a physical body. I continue to explore my inner self and learn the lessons I am here on earth to learn.

CHAPTER 26

NAKED CONFIDENCE

By Elle Bright

The secret of my success? An Australian photographer who gets to work with Gok Wan MBE of "Look Good Naked" fame and has an incredible restored chapel she leases from Prince William and Kate Middleton as her boudoir studio?

My focus and alignment allowed me to break through my Imposter Syndrome. Alignment is everything because you can't focus and keep going when it's not a full mind, body, heart and soul … YES!

So … how did I discover this? Photography was a paid hobby for many years, but when I was 8-months pregnant, my husband's job fell through, and everything changed! And whether it was pregnancy hormones or my usual Aussie madness, I was determined to make my photography a real business.

As an international mining consultant, I was used to stepping out into the unknown, figuring out the science and making it work. I'd been responsible for budgets worth tens of millions. I'd been responsible for people's lives in the desert or the jungle and had a near-death experience myself more than once, and this had given me such extreme confidence that I believed I could surely find a way to make my business soar!

Whilst my son napped, I got to building my photography business even though I had no clue. Full of enthusiasm, I found some clients, but I was scared of showing up and being seen; I was comparing myself with others' success, I felt salesy and couldn't talk about pricing, and my ego was having a field day in procrastination, perfectionism and catastrophising my business's imminent demise! I felt like a failure and an imposter, and I was practically working for free!

So I worked for other photographers and paid gurus, but it wasn't until I applied for a commercial lease, after months of "looking" for a studio, that everything started to take shape. I had finally taken the decisive action to challenge my imposter syndrome and fear of failing. I had finally stopped procrastinating and began taking aligned action, and, yes, the universe tested me with setbacks, but I held true, which led me to discover my studio just 3hrs drive from London.

Through my focused, consistent and aligned action, I learnt how to normalise feeling challenged and unsure, by applying a variety of methodologies like EFT, NLP, practicing gratitude, and more, and I was able to overcome my Imposter Syndrome! I didn't feel like a fake. In fact, I was becoming more "me" every day. Would you believe that I didn't even have a bed for my first photoshoot at my studio? Just a blow-up mattress!

I now know that my naked confidence makes women want to work with me. I know that I'm not the best photographer. Still, I am always improving and have always worked in male-dominated fields. I know how to help women reconnect with their feminine power. As a wife and mother, I know how to help women rediscover their womanliness after years dedicated to child-rearing and caring for others, and I love that I get to help women through coaching and photography or both to overcome their imposter syndrome, because we all deserve to feel fabulous in mind, body, heart and soul.

CHAPTER 27

MOODY BOOTS & BANTER

Ellie LaCrosse

My inspirational success story is aimed at ambitious younger women trying to establish credibility in a male-dominated industry like Construction.

Women in professional roles throughout the industry were rare forty years ago; many women have since joined in trades and technical positions. However, this industry is still heavily male-dominated today. I believe my insights still hold true and have value.

My first Construction lecture at Aston University in Birmingham was an eye-opener. I walked into a stuffy lecture theatre to be met with a hundred pairs of male eyes swivelling around to look at me. I felt like a lonely island of femininity surrounded by sweaty testosterone soup!

Later, in my first real role as a Quantity Surveyor (QS), working on the Queen Elizabeth Crown Courts in Birmingham's City Centre, I had a hilarious but profound incident which shaped how I tried to conduct myself in my working life.

My Director instructed me to visit the site, introduce myself to the Chief Engineer as a courtesy and set up my site office. I duly turned up one bright spring morning, all bedecked in a safety jacket, steel toe-capped boots and the ubiquitous yellow hard hat. I found the Chief Engineer climbing out of a huge culvert, all 6'3" 'man-mountain', covered in smeary mud. I strode up to him, shot my hand out to shake his hand and said, "Hello, I'm Ellie; I'm the new QS!"

Silence. Glowering stare. Curious looks from the trades standing nearby, sensing a showdown. The Chief looked me up and down and, without hinting or irony, said, "Huh! That's all we need on-site, an f-ing engineer with tits!"

Stunned, I computed in my frantic brain that however I responded to this salvo would colour my relationship with this powerful man.

"You're only jealous!" I retorted, looking down at my breasts and turning on my heels to walk towards my office cabin with as much dignity and bravado as I could muster. Giggling tradesmen and wolf-whistles accompanied my walk of shame.

Later, back at my City office, the call came through to visit the MD and explain what had happened on-site.

"So, Ellie, what exactly happened on site today? Must be a record for being on-site, what, 60 seconds, and pissing off the Chief? He called to complain of your cheekiness!" he barked.

I recounted verbatim the exchange with the Chief. My MD rubbed his shoulders like I was an annoying burden. I held my breath.

Then he let out a huge laugh, "Oh good grief, give him hell. You did right, bat away the brickbats with sarcasm, remember you've got to work with this man indirectly, so try not to start a war, please?" he smirked. Relief flooded through me, and I felt he had my back personally with the firm's support. It was a great life lesson in successfully managing relationships without being constantly offended and outraged.

I used to mentor younger female colleagues, and my mantra was, 'Use your wits and humour to deflate those put-downs.' Banter earns respect and beats prejudice!

CHAPTER 28

BECOMING ME – A LOVE STORY

By Gill Davidson

I always went for the bad boys, unavailable men and men I thought I could save.

These men, though, found it difficult to express themselves emotionally; men who didn't respect me, didn't treat me properly and were jealous of my son.

I made excuses for black eyes, chipped teeth, for bruised and cut lips. That was only in one relationship. For some reason, I didn't learn, though. The next one, the next relationship, he appeared like a knight in shining armour.

He bought me flowers, took me out to lunch, and made me laugh. For a while, I seemed to have the perfect relationship. When I look back, though, I did keep getting a niggling feeling that something wasn't right. He rarely stayed over, and when he did, it was the same evening every week, always Wednesdays.

Funnily enough, although maybe not, my mum said to me that something wasn't right almost three months into the relationship. I chose to ignore her, even though I knew she was right.

He'd told me that he and his wife were separated and were going through a divorce, and I believed him. But we do things like that, don't we? We choose to believe what we want to believe.

We ignore those things we think or know will cause us pain.

The lies, the deceit, the manipulation, the coming and going continued for 10 years. I used to be ashamed to admit that. I used to feel foolish, naive and gullible when I thought back to that time.

The lies this man told, the things he blamed me for when they were absolutely nothing to do with me and had happened before we'd even met, was an experience that eventually took its toll on my mental health. I became extremely unwell, struggling with anxiety, depression, panic attacks, and suicidal thoughts.

I had counselling with three or four different counsellors and took four different lots of antidepressants during that 10 years. Strangely, or maybe not, I'd never been on antidepressants or needed counselling before that, and I've never needed either since.

The counselling and antidepressants did help me to some extent. Still, they didn't help me with my massively low self-esteem, lack of confidence and massive distrust of men.

I desperately wanted to have a relationship with a man I could trust, a relationship where we could work together and support each other. I knew, though, that I would need to do some serious work on myself to have the relationship I yearned for.

I made the decision to really get to know myself, to understand what was important to me and what made me feel happy and fulfilled.

My success was making the decision to become who I really was. I knew by making that decision to work on myself, never again would I settle for something that wasn't good for me, and never again would I put myself through torture and torment in the name of love.

It would take a whole book to tell you about that relationship and how it impacted me negatively rather than positively. Maybe one day I'll write that book.

CHAPTER 29

LEARNING TO LOVE MYSELF

By Gill Routledge

I now love my life and have developed a deep connection to myself, my husband and my family. It hasn't always felt this way because unwittingly, circumstances in my life resulted in shutting down and closing off to the possibility of being loved or loving another, including myself.

Learning to love myself was not something that I suddenly woke up one morning and put on my to-do list or set of goals for my life. It was a gradual unravelling, sometimes gentle and often came with huge wake-up calls.

I want to share part of my story so that other women may relate to and share some simple skills and practices that I have used and continue to use daily.

Firstly, I feel it is vital to reflect on how childhood experiences influence our relationship with ourselves and others. Shedding light on specific tendencies enables us to make different choices, break free from debilitating behaviours and drop into a place of stillness and peace.

This has facilitated an awakening to a more joyful and creative life in which I have grown to build healthier relationships with my family and myself— a life where my work makes a real difference. My emotions are a trusted guide towards continuous and deeper learning about who I am. This was not always the case. I witnessed violence and verbal abuse in my childhood, adopted strategies that didn't serve me in later years and experienced deep depression.

I grew up witnessing my father's eruptions of anger and my mother's emotional outbursts. On one occasion, this left me feeling stuck in a warzone where no one would win, and any survivors would be scarred forever. Communicating how I felt seemed futile, and I felt helpless to change anything. Internally something was screaming inside, wanting my parents to wake up and see what was important. It was as if, at that moment, the breath seemed gripped in a vice, and the body froze. This seemed to imprint a pattern to freeze or run each time I felt myself in a conflict.

Like many women, I learned to earn love and respect by doing things that would please my parents. As a result, other people's needs always came before mine, which led to a sense of unworthiness, lack of self-respect and, ultimately, depression. It doesn't have to be this way, and there is a solution.

As a child, my go-to place of escape was to find solace in nature, which still offers a nurturing and safe place of peace and solitude. Writing and making time to be still and meditate is the simplest and yet has been the most difficult practice to adopt and is my saving grace.

Writing is one of the best ways to express thoughts and feelings and a gift many of us have put on hold because commitments take precedence. Adopting a regular meditation practice connects us to our heart and inner sense of who we truly are, which, in essence, is love.

CHAPTER 30

MY EPIPHANY BUSINESS

By Helen Helliwell

After leaving school and working in many different roles, I had no thought of ever running my own business. Getting divorced, marrying again and getting divorced a second time reinforced my need for security and a salaried, regular paying job.

However, sometimes life throws you the most unexpected situations. I was finally in a permanent relationship I wanted to last forever, but I had been in a challenging salaried role, faced with an untenable situation. I decided to fulfil a dream, with my partner's full support, to work in emergency services on the frontline. It seemed crazy thinking at the time!

I had never gone into fitness training, and I needed to pass fitness tests - at the age of 39! It was the most intense period, juggling a job, child, house, partner, studying and regular workouts. I used to loathe treadmills, hated the thought of lactic acid, getting hot and sticky, out of breath, and constantly tired. There were many times I felt like giving up. The only way I could cope mentally was to cover screens, stare out of windows and focus on something totally different, willing time to go by.

Was it worth it? 1000%!!

I passed all 7 of my fitness tests.

However, I had never really appreciated making marriage work when working 24-hour rotating shifts – just 3 days off in a year were the same.

So, my epiphany moment arrived!!

While training for those fitness tests, with other people watching this mad woman skipping 300 skips in three minutes, running on a treadmill staring out the window intently, using the weights, abdominal work and another exercise three times a week, the seed was sown in my mind. I decided to apply myself again and studied like mad to qualify for the highest level possible. My determination paid off, and now 18 years later, I am still doing this work.

My business, BHB Health and Fitness, is focused on guiding, coaching, supporting and achieving the best possible health, wellness, fitness, toning, and energised bodies and minds for anyone who needs it. I usually work with ladies around 40-70, but no one is excluded.

The wonderful clients I have seen over the years have achieved the health they only dreamed of, prevented lifestyle-related illness, and managed pre-existing conditions, all in my very healthy environment. Even with the pandemic restrictions, it did not stop us; we trained in open spaces, much to the amusement of dog walkers passing by.

So why is it successful? Because I believe in business, you must be passionate, businesslike, thoughtful, treat others how you want to be treated, be respectful, and always remember you are only as good as your effort.

Would I change anything over the last 18 years – you can only learn from history and be the best person you can going forward. Always willing to learn, improve your skills, offer the best possible service to all your clients and deliver every minute of your working time.

CHAPTER 31

THINK AGAIN: IT'S A PROCESS

By Jasmine Mbye

I sat there in a room filled with things that were not mine. I'd left my toxic and abusive relationship and was in a refuge with my little one. Plus, I'd paused another business. This is an example of when it's easy to feel like a failure. However, I didn't because I decided to reframe failure some years ago. I wouldn't allow myself to believe that I could be a failure. That's right, I decided to believe that I couldn't fail; only the things I tried could fail. And I gave myself permission to fail at what I tried. Failure is evidence of trying, and we fail our way to success.

Another critical thing I've done on this journey is follow my Triple-A Process: Affirmations, Action, and Accountability. The process has been a gradual realisation. I started with Affirmations years ago, which took me from self-loathing to self-loving, from looking in the mirror with disgust to liking who and what I saw. Daily affirmations are a significant key to success in every area of life.

Affirmations are positive statements we make about ourselves and our life, such as 'I am capable'. Before winning my awards, each morning and night, I declared, 'I am an award-winning entrepreneur'. Anything we repeatedly hear, we come to believe, as it enters into our subconscious minds enabling us to reprogramme our beliefs. Many studies have shown this. So create some positively worded statements in line with your dreams and desires and say them at the start and end of the day and whenever negative, self-defeating thoughts come.

I later learned that Affirmations are just the beginning. The next stage is to take action. Our action stage can be a mixture of planned and inspired steps. I was open to opportunities which allowed me to work to get recognised, like doing a TEDx, and then put myself forward as a potential candidate for award nominations. Without these actions, I wouldn't be writing this after becoming a multi-award-winning Speaker less than 18 months after leaving the refuge.

Consider what actions you can take that are in line with manifesting your affirmations. Commit to taking some planned and inspired action when the opportunity is presented.

(You'll be surprised at what will present itself once you commit). Ideally, we'll take action every day, which moves towards making real those things we dream of and desire.

Taking action is likely to lead you outside your comfort zone, hence why we need the final stage in the process; Accountability. Who will hold us accountable? Who will check in to see how we're getting on and what we've achieved? Who can we trust to be cheerleaders or disciplinarians when needed? Success isn't achieved in isolation; it takes collaboration. We just need two or three people to support us. It's best if those people have some experience or exposure to what we're on the road to achieving. I was accountable to a mentorship group.

This reframing of failure and following the Triple-A Process has empowered me to overcome toxicity and abuse as a child and partner, along with business failure. Now I'm in my home, surrounded by my things, in a healthier relationship and with a successful business.

I am successful not because of what I have but because of who I have become.

CHAPTER 32

FROM HIGHS TO LOWS AND BACK AGAIN

By Joanne Outram

I'm sure you know what it means to be financially successful. I thought I did, believing I had made it when my business hit 7 figures, I was travelling the world in business class, and I owned both a Porsche and a Mercedes. However, as I found out, success can be a fleeting thing. And just as quickly as I thought I had arrived, the property market crashed, and an ex-employee set out to destroy my business, sending me into a financial tailspin.

The climb to financial success is often slow and steady, but the fall can be fast and brutal. And as anyone who has hit rock bottom will tell you, it can be a wake-up call. I faced a choice: stay stuck or build again, this time with a foundation that would give me peace of mind.

This was also my opportunity to evaluate what was truly important to me, free from the influence of what others had or thought I should have. And I realized that I had never truly evaluated my core values. So, I set about changing my mindset. I knew that if I wanted different results, I needed other inputs. And the one major component I could change was how I thought about money and success.

How did I turn my financial situation around and achieve an abundant mindset? My formula is to take good old-fashioned action in the following areas:

Assessed my situation: I took a close look at my financial situation, identified the sources of the problems, and made a plan to address them. Luckily, I had the skills to do this, but you can seek help from a financial coach or accountant.

Prioritised my spending: I focused on what was necessary for the business to function and to cover my personal needs.

Increased revenue: I looked for ways to improve my income, including expanding my services and raising prices. I also took a part-time job to ensure I had a consistent income.

Stayed positive: Maintaining a positive and confident attitude was essential. Therefore, I surrounded myself with supportive people and avoided negative thinking.

Focused on abundance: I cultivated an abundance mindset by focusing on what I had rather than what I lacked. I was grateful for what had been achieved and focused on future opportunities for growth and success.

The key is to stay committed to the process and be patient, as results can take some time.

Finally, I experienced financial success again but this time, with stability. It's not just about the numbers in the bank but the peace of mind that comes with it. As my thinking became more abundant, it gave me the confidence, optimism, and creativity to approach my business in a way that aligned with my values.

Embracing an abundant mindset (the belief that there are enough resources, opportunities, and success to go around) is essential for small business owners like me. It allows us to believe that our businesses can succeed, that our market is big enough, and that we have the potential to grow and expand.

And whether you're in business or not, I hope you can achieve financial success in a way that brings you peace and joy.

CHAPTER 33

DIGGING DEEP: CONQUERING YOUR DEMONS

By Joanne Parker

What can a middle-aged woman from Yorkshire possibly have in common with a Greek hero and a British eighteenth-century romantic poet?

The answer – we have all swam the Hellespont. Something that, even today, only a small group of people can claim to have done.

The Hellespont, also known as the Dardanelles, is a narrow stretch of water that links Europe and Asia in the northwest of Turkey. This ordinarily crowded shipping lane is closed for ninety minutes one day a year to allow a race to take place to commemorate Turkish Remembrance Day.

On 30 August 2008, I joined 229 other people from all over the world to participate in the race and attempt to swim the 4.5km across the Dardanelles.

Up to this point, I had no experience of open water swimming. I was overweight and unfit.

The swimming gave me something positive to focus on. My husband of twenty-one years was dying of skin cancer. I didn't know then, but he would only survive one more year.

My friend Jenny and I trained for two or three months. Graduating from my local public baths to the outdoor lido and then to the sea. Swimming in open water means you can't put your feet down and touch the bottom! That was when the magnitude of what we were doing hit home. How would I cope? What dangers lurked in the water below? Eventually, the day of the race dawned.

All alone, miles from anywhere

On the first whistle, most swimmers headed off into the sea. They were the racers, the front crawlers who were there to complete the race as quickly as possible. Jenny and I were in the second group, the breaststrokers. Equally determined, but not as fast!

Although we set off in a group, before long, I found myself alone in open water with just the jellyfish for company. At the start, orange swimming hats bobbed around as far as the eye could see. Suddenly I was on my own. That was when the panic set in. How long had I been in the water? Had I gone the wrong way? I had no way of knowing. Why could I not see anyone else?

I persevered. I thought about my husband back home and what he was dealing with. However scared I was at that moment was nothing to what he was feeling. My horizon was slowly coming into view, but what did he see ahead of him?

Success - I completed the swim in 76 minutes and got a certificate to prove it. I also raised over £1000 in sponsorship for Cancer Research. I went home incredibly proud and fortified for what lay ahead.

In October 2009, I said goodbye to my husband.

Conquering my fears, embracing the challenge of that open water swim and facing up to my demons enabled me to move forward. Whenever I doubt my ability to cope, I think back to that lonely woman in the middle of the sea. I know I can succeed, whatever life offers.

CHAPTER 34

SIMPLY THE BREAST

By Joanne Taylor

His breathing was soft and sweet, his warm body against mine, skin to skin, I could feel the love and connection building, and within minutes he was reaching for my breast. I felt nervous but excited all at the same time, and then it happened, the start of our breastfeeding journey.

I'm fairly confident that most readers first thought was that of surprise. Apologies for disappointing you, but it highlights how society portrays a woman's body. Sexualising the breasts in a way that women do not feel comfortable doing the one thing our breasts were biologically functioned to do, produce milk to feed our babies.

I am a mother of three, and it was my choice to breastfeed them. In total, I have fed for just over 4 years. Each journey was unique. We faced many hurdles, including mastitis, cracked nipples, thrush, tongue tie, feeding aversions, oversupply, engorgement and the most challenging of all, a baby who could not suck. I did not even know that was a thing. It was certainly never discussed in my antenatal classes, but yes, I gave birth to a baby with no sucking reflex. He was just as confused as I was, but I quickly had to learn how to hand express into a syringe. It was exhausting and not only physically demanding but mentally and emotionally draining too.

I had no idea how something so natural could be so hard. What I was confident about, though, was my determination to make it work, and I did. I faced challenges along the way, but instead of seeing them as a way out, I used them as lessons; I realised that this was the most rewarding thing I had ever done, giving me purpose. My purpose was to feed and nourish my baby; the reward was watching them grow, knowing I was wholly responsible for that.

My passion for breastfeeding led me to train as a volunteer breastfeeding support worker. I spent time in the postnatal ward advising and supporting new mums.

I was always the first one there when my friends had babies, and I loved being able to support them at such a personal time of their life.

One thing that kept coming up when I would chat with mums was that they often felt unsupported in their choices. Not entirely just their choice to breastfeed, but every decision they made as a mother was being questioned by those closest to her. It really saddened me as I knew with the proper support and encouragement, they would flourish with the confidence every mother deserves to have. The anxiety and fear of judgement from others is one of the main reasons mothers give up breastfeeding. In fact, less than 1% of women who breastfeed do so after their baby is 12 months old, and the UK has the lowest breastfeeding rate in the world.

My advice to others would be to educate yourself so you can ignore the negative opinions of others and have the belief in yourself that you can overcome and achieve. Normalising breastfeeding to inspire future generations is empowering. Embrace your breasts and own your story.

CHAPTER 35

CO-PARENTING WELL: VIOLENCE TO GOOD VIBES

By Julia Hollenbery

I was 38 when I met him and 42 when I had a baby as a single mum. I was happy to be a Mum, but our parental relationship was a mess. Lots of volatile arguments. Not what I wanted to bring a baby into. We split up whilst I was pregnant, and then my Mum died.

A lot was going on then.

Today my daughter's Dad and I are friends. We co-parent well, and she's a happy, confident, kind girl, head of her year at secondary school. In fact, we three are going away together for her upcoming 13th birthday. I'm glad and proud of our collective success. Caroline is equally at home in both of her homes.

I'd like to share what helped me:

Our parenting was not an overnight success, but slowly and steadily, prioritising our daughter's wellbeing, we've forged something beautiful, full of love, integrity and boundaries. What helps is being in service to love. Putting someone else first, not life all about me, me, me.

We allowed space and time. After the first six months, I was mostly alone with the baby (an experience that felt like every day lasted a year!) Caroline would see her Dad each week. We allowed an hour for her movement between us. As a baby born too quickly by caesarean, I understood she'd need extra transition time. (By contrast, at the house next door, the Mum's car would screech up, the horn would honk, and she'd yell to the Dad, "Send him out!") I let Caroline's Dad garden our front yard, therapy for him, and he created a beautiful space we often met in. What helps is slow spaciousness for feelings to be felt, eyes to be looked into, and conversations to happen.

Like every parent, we learnt on the job - creating birthday celebrations, taking her to playgroup, then primary school, and figuring out routines and finances. I still got triggered. What really helps is taking responsibility for feelings and behaviour. I 'owned' my stuff rather than blaming or collapsing. I also understood that for a child, it's ok to see their parents fighting, so long as they see them making up. Children learn discomfort is part of life, and communication requires care.

What helps is trusting our intuition. Listening to the spontaneous wisdom of the body. I love to notice what it's telling us. Magical moments arose from us listening to our bodily intelligence. In one instance, this illogical but strongly felt sense saved our daughter's life.

Self-care is vital. Doing what's needed for myself. Not for my child or our parental relationship: Meditation. Exercise. Creating order. Drinking water. And more. I drew myself a colourful table pinned to the wall, listing habits I could satisfyingly tick off when each was achieved. Remembering, I am a woman, not just a mum.

Our success gave me peace in my soul. I love my ex and respect him as a friend, co-parent and individual. I've learnt to learn not just with him but also from him. This peacefulness gave me space to write my book, published last year, The Healing Power of Pleasure: Seven Medicines for Rediscovering the Innate Joy of Being, and to create a new loving, intimate relationship with my boyfriend. I'm happy, grateful and fulfilled.

CHAPTER 36

HOW TO BE HAPPY

By Julie Leonard

I used to look for happiness in all the wrong places.

As a child and teenager, and even in my 20s, I was an anxious, sensitive worrier with very little self-esteem. I never felt good enough or that my opinion counted, and I truly believed I was the ugliest woman in the world.

At school, I was shy and was bullied and picked upon by both kids and teachers. I wasn't popular and felt like I didn't fit in. At University (it will come as no surprise that I studied Psychology), I found people I connected with but struggled with anxiety and low confidence. I couldn't even walk into the cafeteria on my own. I was so nervous!

When a long-term negative relationship ended in my early 30s, I finally had the time, space and tools to transform myself and my life. I remember clearly sitting on my sofa one day. I was low in mood, emotionally exhausted and feeling alone. I was confident in my job (I had a flourishing career in mental health), but apart from work, I felt unhappy and unfulfilled in my life. Sitting on my sofa, it was then that I had a moment that changed my life.

I asked myself, 'WHAT IS SCARIER? Staying as I am or facing my fears and putting myself out there?" The realisation was that I was more scared to stay in the life I had.

To remain stuck and unfulfilled. My transformation began.

It wasn't until I turned my attention inwards that change happened. I have been on a continual journey of transformation and growth, and I've trained in many life-changing techniques. I used MBSR to break my cycle of negative thinking, self-compassion meditation to get rid of my inner critic and create a kind and compassionate inner voice and loving-kindness meditation and gratitude to cultivate a practice of compassion and kindness towards myself and others. This inner work changed my mindset, improved my confidence and resilience and increased my happiness. I discovered that when I became intentional about my life, so much was in my control.

At 40, I found love

At 42, I moved country

At 43, I had a baby

At 44, I started my own business

At 48, I spoke at my first International Event

At 49, I published my first book

At 50, I got married

In my 20's and 30s, I told myself, 'I'm not good enough. 'Today I ask myself, 'What do I want to achieve next?'

I'm on a mission to change the lives of women all around the world. Through my company Julie Leonard Coaching and my group coaching programmes, I help women to shed the limiting beliefs that hold them back, to step into their full potential and be truly happy.

It's never too late to create the life you want. Your life and your happiness are within your control.

CHAPTER 37

FROM TEA MAKER TO BUSINESS OWNER

By Karen Bengall

I went through school not really having a clear idea of what I wanted to do with my life once I was out in the big wide world; however, I did know that I wanted to do 'something' creative. Whilst all of my friends left school to pursue an office or bank-type career, I knew that just wasn't for me. I simply wasn't destined for a desk job, that much I knew.

So in July 1990, aged 18, I started my career in photography, working for a Fine Art Photographer as an assistant. By that, I mean a tea maker, a film runner, and a bag carrier, but that was O.K. I had no previous experience, so it was only right I learnt from the bottom and fought my way up through the company. Based in Mayfair, the company worked with art dealers and auction houses, from expensive jewellery to priceless Old Master paintings; the work was varied, my colleagues were fun to work with, and I learnt so much, including how to make tea for the photographers!

By 2013, I was still at the same company. But things had changed... the company was a lot smaller by now, and with new owners on board, it wasn't the same 'fun' place to work anymore. I started to do more and more private work on the side, and I realised I was using all my holiday to cover it, but I was scared to go self-employed. However, at this time in my life, my dad was diagnosed with Parkinson's, and to see him deteriorate from this larger-than-life man into a shell of his former self, broke my heart and made me realise we just don't know what lies around the corner in life, and this is not a dress rehearsal. So I handed in my notice in and set off on my journey of self-employment.

It's been 10 years since I started working for myself, and there have been plenty of challenges along the way. From a global pandemic to a recession, I won't say it's been easy; I still have days or weeks where I question what I am doing. Running your own solo business can also be incredibly lonely, with no one to talk to over your problems or the struggles ahead. But I am extremely proud of myself and what I have achieved.

I wouldn't want to return to earning money from someone else's pocket; besides, I am probably too long in the tooth now to be employable.

I have my own studio now in Kent. With videography added to my services, I plan to create an educational platform next. It would be great to teach others the skillset I have learnt and help those who want to improve their photography or create their own video. From understanding light, and your equipment, to learning how to compose the shot and run a business, I feel it's time to give something back.

Besides, it doesn't get any easier carrying cases and equipment on location jobs now, so maybe a desk job doesn't sound that bad.

Thank you for reading my story.

CHAPTER 38

THE BEGGAR CHILDREN OF KANDY

By Karen Burge

Sitting in a cafe people watching is always fascinating. That day in the dusty town of Kandy in Sri Lanka was no exception. My husband and I had moved to Sri Lanka with our three-month-old daughter just as the civil war had broken out, and this was a weekend treat.

Looking out of the window, I noticed the beggar women sitting in the shade with their children, and it struck me that those children weren't at school. They were just listlessly sitting around.

Watching them, the seed of an idea was sown to try and get these children off the streets and give them a better chance. However, I was new, white and female, and it wasn't my culture. If anything was to happen, I needed allies. We rented a house from an American missionary family who had returned to the States for two years. It was immediately obvious that Archdeacon Ratanayake, at their church, was the person to get onside.

He was thrilled to get involved! My idea was to provide them with a meal, a wash, and clean clothes, and most importantly, activities and some rudimentary education. If the mothers knew their children were getting these free benefits, they would happily let them attend.

Soon Archdeacon Ratanayake found a small, unused chapel. It was basic, it needed clearing out and smartening up, but it would do.

There was a main room, a smaller one that would serve as a kitchen and a toilet and a place to shower.

Then I approached the school in England where my husband had taught and asked for help. Two months later, we excitedly drove six hours to Colombo to fetch two tea chests full of clothes, books and equipment.

Meanwhile, I'd found a cook and a wonderful lady called Victoria. I applied to ActionHelp2000, and they sent Lindsay, a tall, pale girl with boundless energy and patience.

Kandy Children's Centre was launched, and every day 30 children turned up, eager to make the most of this opportunity. I still have photos showing their smiling faces as they ate a good meal, splashed around in the shower, played, and learnt to read and write.

There were problems, of course; red tape, a caretaker who thought he was onto a good thing, and others who thought we were crazy helping these children they considered worthless. Two years after we returned home, Save The Children Fund took it over, and it ran successfully for many years. That is my success.

But what did I learn from it?

I could have spent my days as an ex-pat, attending coffee mornings and looking after my baby, but there are always people who need you, and like the beggar children of Kandy, they will drive you. There will be obstacles, but you just have to keep going. Find your purpose, but importantly, find people to help you along the way. Success comes in many forms, and few achieve it on their own.

CHAPTER 39

SUCCESS – ON PURPOSE

By Katie Farrell

My greatest success took decades of hoping and almost never happened.

From a young age, I'd wanted to be a mum and presumed I would be. However, in my mid-20s, that dream was dealt a crushing blow. On my lunch break one day, I received a phone call from my GP with life-changing news: "We have your blood results here…you have Poly Cystic Ovarian Syndrome (PCOS)…affects fertility…struggle to conceive…."

I don't recall anything more of that conversation. I remember feeling time had suddenly stood still while the world started closing in around me. A deafening ringing filled my ears. It felt like someone had stabbed me through the heart.

How could this be happening? Never conceive? Never be a mum!

I froze, not knowing how to process the news.

It didn't help that I was newly single, just out of a long-term relationship and started questioning my decision. Should I have stayed? What is this cruel karma?

However, it didn't take long for my maternal instincts to kick in. I started researching PCOS. One of the common answers I discovered was that there's no cure.

PCOS is a syndrome, meaning there's no direct known cause for the symptoms. So all the medical world can do is manage those symptoms, which include irregular or absent periods, insulin resistance, weight gain and infertility.

I tried many medications and treatments over the years, including Metformin to manage the hypoglycaemic attacks, the pill, diets, and various complementary therapies. Each seemed to have certain levels of success, but generally only temporary and often accompanied by side effects.

When I was introduced to Reiki, things finally started to shift. Reiki is a form of energy healing, channelling universal energy through specially attuned practitioners' hands to the client to treat physical and emotional issues. I loved the experiences, feeling the energy coursing through me and 'seeing' visualisations that I knew I could not have generated consciously. My practitioner told me I had a gift with energy, and I knew I had to do this!

I qualified as a Reiki Practitioner, and whilst I was proud of this achievement, it was the by-product that blew me away - I'd fallen pregnant! From feelings of dread when my returned periods suddenly stopped to the overwhelming joy at seeing the blue line appear on the pregnancy test, I felt like all my dreams had finally come true!

I went on to qualify for Reiki Level II and a month later achieved my greatest success: becoming mum to a healthy 9lb son!

15 years, a spiritual awakening and lots of energetic development later, I learned that being a mum was a major part of my soul purpose. Now I help others align to their soul purpose, heal from any obstacles in their way and achieve their greatest successes – whatever those look like.

CHAPTER 40

MY INVESTMENT IN PERSONAL GROWTH

By Kazlina Burroughs

For thirty-one years, I worked in a very trusted role, ensuring everything was done legitimately for private clients, corporate companies and other banks, including anti-money laundering, whilst holding a position at a leading global investment banking firm. Yet, I now feel more successful than ever!

My role at the bank was very challenging, and I thrived under pressure. I was able to learn quickly and think on my feet. I am a people person, so I was considered as bringing fun to work and acting as the "mummy manager." I enjoyed my time at the bank and never thought about personal development in my private life.

Then one day, I was invited to attend a big event that changed my life forever. It was a Tony Robbins experience. That was when I had a lightbulb moment, and I never looked back. I was between contracts with the bank, so I decided to learn about therapy and coaching.

I became a Master NLP Practitioner and Hypnotherapist. I then invested in understanding how to start a business while practicing my skills and gaining more knowledge. I began to feel more experienced until I eventually reached a point where my friend suggested that I help others.

Once again, I had to start my career from the ground up after so many years at the bank.

I explored a role as a therapist and started working as a Support Worker for disabled and neurodiverse people.

When I supported one individual in their own home, the family was so impressed that they asked me to become their family's personal assistant. I then founded my business, Burroughs PA Support.

I had seen a gap in the market for personal assistants that could help families who needed personal support. Now my clients melt my heart. My success is helping the people I support reach their potential and achieve their own success. My clients are now able to do things they never thought possible.

It takes someone like me to show them that they can dream bigger, set new goals, and reach higher. I was not schooled from twelve and had no qualifications at eighteen. However, I have become an entrepreneur with fantastic work experience that got me where I am today. Believing in yourself is so important. When you believe in yourself and work hard, things will fall into place.

Years ago, I thought my success in the city was due to luck, but I have learnt that my commitment and dedication got me to a manager level, and I ran many projects with my own staff. I've learned that no one can tell you about your capabilities except yourself. When you believe in yourself and work hard, things will fall into place.

Success is something that you define for yourself. You set your own standards and decide when you've reached them.

CHAPTER 41

MY LIFE, MY CHOICE

By Kim Lengling

Time to pull up my big-girl panties. That was my main thought when life took an unexpected shift.

Mind-numbing fatigue. Each day, I felt as if I was walking through deep water. Thoughts were a struggle to keep together, weight loss, hair loss, and scaly skin. Something wasn't right.

Doctor appointments; so many doctor appointments and tests. Frustration, exhaustion, and feeling ill began to deplete my mental resources, making me feel worse. Finally, my initial diagnosis was Type 2 Diabetes, but my symptoms continued to worsen. So, I find myself, once again, watching as a needle goes into my vein for another round of bloodwork.

This round is sent to a specialist with a final diagnosis of LADA-Diabetes, and I find myself insulin dependent. Studies report that about 10% of adults initially diagnosed with clinical Type 2 diabetes (T2D) have LADA.

From the onset of symptoms to the final diagnosis was approximately one year.

Before being diagnosed, working full-time outside the home became physically challenging. I had to request a leave of absence, then COVID hit, and the world changed. My job soon became nonexistent, and I wondered what I would do to maintain my house and home while learning to deal with a life-altering medical diagnosis.

Over time, although stressful and frustrating, I began to see a shift in my mindset. I decided to make my own "job" and investigated ways to work from home.

I noticed how I exercised, used my time, and viewed and ate food. Everything now revolved around when I ate and how I ate, with Insulin pens at the ready. As a result, I had to make drastic changes to keep a healthy balance between my physical and mental health.

I did begin working from home, making my way on my terms. I began to look at food differently. Instead of saying, "I've never cared for that." I now say, "If I mix in a little of this or that, this dish could be yummy." I created a routine that fit my new lifestyle and that included a new mindset.

Mindset plays a large part in how our daily lives work. For example, choosing to wake up grumpy because you don't feel well can affect your entire day. Choosing to wake up with the mindset of, "Okay, I'm not feeling great this morning; let's set different goals for today and crush them."

I've learned to rest when my body tells me to rest. I've learned to set boundaries and stick to them. I've learned that it is okay to consider myself the focus.

It wasn't easy to shift from being constantly on the go, ignoring what my body was telling me, to being fully aware of what my body was telling me and adjusting my day accordingly.

Now in my second year of living with LADA-Diabetes and having a home-based business, I can honestly say that despite the days I may feel unwell, each day is an opportunity to make a difference, either in my own life or in someone else's. The choice is mine.

How are you choosing to face each day?

CHAPTER 42

RISK TO BELIEVE OR BELIEVE TO RISK?

By Kinga Stabryla

Women are often suggested to be complicit, agreeable, and nurturing. Although these traits are beneficial in some areas of our lives, they do not naturally serve us well when starting a business.

The media portrays business as a risky enterprise, and studies show entrepreneurs who take risks are more likely to succeed. Alongside the scary statistic of how 90% of start-ups fail in the first two years along with gender disparities, this is hardly encouraging. Why would you start a business? You see, the secret to good risk-taking is calculating, managing, and believing in it - though which one comes first is like the chicken and the egg scenario. It is all about balance, and the last time I checked, females were the queens of balancing. Business is similar, even though you make decisions based on market understanding, competition, and potential rewards.

For a long time, the thought of taking risks and potentially failing held me back, despite being told that I was on the right path to success. I was too concerned with validation and acceptance from the wrong people. Eventually, I realised that no one else would control my life but myself.

The turning point came when I received a lowball job offer after working for just travel expenses whilst trying to prove my value to companies like Microsoft, Twitter, and Amazon for a few months.

I decided that enough was enough, and I was not going to wait for validation and permission to pursue my passions and dreams. Most importantly, I did not want to be taken advantage of any longer.

After saying my goodbyes to being an employee, at just 22, my business was, unbeknownst to me, starting. I wasn't sure how or why, but all I knew was that I would now be in control of my destiny and be my biggest cheerleader. It is safe to say that this risk paid off – after all, I risked years putting my life under other people's control, so now it was my turn.

Entrepreneurship was born! I had no prior marketing experience or business connections. I relied on my transferable skills, wit, and faith to succeed. Taking consistent small steps forward led to business success. In my first year, I assisted a multi-millionaire, a billionaire, and a law firm with various aspects of their marketing and personal brand development. I, a young immigrant female from a northern public school, first to go to university and start a business.

Now, there are several strategies you can use to increase your comfort levels when taking risks:

- Reframe: Consider reframing the risk as an opportunity or challenge rather than a threat.
- Information: Seek information and advice from trusted sources to increase understanding of the situation and reduce uncertainty.
- Plan: Create a plan for any damage control, anticipate challenges and consider different outcomes and how to respond.
- Self-confidence: Engage in activities that take you out of your comfort zone.
- Support: Seek out supportive friends, family members, or mentors who can provide encouragement and support when taking risks.
- Practice: Start with small, manageable risks. Then gradually build up your risk-taking.
- Fail: By failing, you are learning. Fail often.

In short, risk to believe and believe to risk.

CHAPTER 43

MY CHANGING DEFINITION THROUGH THE YEARS

By Lara Cope

Over the last few years of my life, my view of what success is has evolved and radically changed. For me, success is something that I must feel deep within myself. Ten years ago, my idea of success was becoming an Orthopaedic Consultant Surgeon. From my first day in the operating theatre, I felt a deep sense of purpose and passion for this work when I picked up a scalpel.

I knew this was the career path I wanted to pursue, and nothing would stop me from achieving this goal. However, I have always pushed myself to the limit. I now know that one of my previous behaviour patterns was to make things as difficult as possible for myself. I did this without even realising it. I was also filled with self-doubt, imposter syndrome, and a crippling fear of what others thought of me.

As I entered my thirties, I soon realised that trying to have a baby was, in fact, the hardest thing I had ever tried to do. It was the highest mountain I had to climb.

After spending years obsessed with my career, I never really thought twice about when I wanted to have children. I just assumed it would happen when the time was right. I never realised that I had taken my body for granted. I had often lost sleep, was stressed, overworked, didn't exercise, didn't eat right, or didn't eat, all in pursuing a career that I loved.

I had my first failed IVF cycle, my second, my mum got diagnosed with breast cancer, and then I broke. On that day, suddenly, the penny dropped. I may never be a mother. It was too late now. I took a year out of my surgical training to undergo IVF treatment. Unfortunately, it was also the year that the Covid pandemic struck, and the world paused.

I had to cope with these emotions, the other stresses I put on myself, and the stress of my job. I started looking into mindset work but couldn't find a coach that I resonated with. I saw a Facebook advert to train as a certified coach, which changed my life. It not only helped me during my IVF journey but also made me see all the stress I put myself through. I had been so close to burnout, and I didn't realise I had been living my life wrapped in fear, stress, and anxiety.

Success to me now is my beautiful daughter, who brings me an overwhelming sense of joy and fulfilment every single day.

I have now made it my mission to help other stressed-out, overworked, and overwhelmed women live the stress-free lives they truly deserve. I want to empower others to find success and joy in their lives.

CHAPTER 44

IT'S ALL ABOUT LOVE

By Laura Billingham

Why am I choosing to write about love in a book entitled "The Secrets of Successful Women"?

Well, without sounding overly mushy and romantic, one thing I have learned in my almost sixty years on this planet is that love really does drive everything.

Love is at the heart of humanity - even the "bad stuff" wars, murders, rapes, and attacks stem originally from the perpetrator's hatred…and without love, there could be no hate - could there?

Mainstream media, by which I mean TV, movies, magazines and the like, tend to concentrate on love stories between romantic partners. But love is SO much more than that between two adults who choose to spend their life together (or part of it, at least!). For a long time, I also believed that love was primarily connected with our intimate relationships.

I've had several long-term relationships, one of which produced two gorgeous daughters, and each time I truly believed "this was the one"; here was the person I would spend the rest of my life with.

When these relationships failed, I blamed myself…I wasn't good enough, thin enough, gorgeous enough, clever enough, or rich enough.

I never stopped believing in love as a concept - but what I failed to learn was that loving myself had to come first; I'd been brought up (like many of us) to think that as a woman, I should be selfless and put other people's needs ahead of my own.

To quote the character Captain Alberto Bertorelli from "Allo Allo", What a mistake-a to make-a!

I was in my forties before I understood that if I wasn't happy with and in myself and able to prioritise my own needs, it was highly unlikely that I could forge and maintain a relationship with someone else.

That realisation, coupled with an innate knowing that love is at the centre of everything we do as humans - both good AND bad - ultimately led me to explore what I really wanted to do with my life. I rediscovered writing, something I loved (there's that word again!) as a child but had set aside as an adult because it "wouldn't pay the bills".

I took the time to explore the inner me and reconnected with my deeply spiritual side (not religious) that I'd hidden for years because other people may have thought I was "weird". And in doing so, I found a whole new tribe who accepted me as me.

Finding the time and space to love myself opened my eyes and allowed me to connect in a new relationship in ways I had been unable to do in every other previous significant partnership.

Loving myself led to my career change.

Loving myself allowed me to truly love and accept a new partner.

Without love, we cannot be successful women - love drives everything.

And that is the reason I chose to write about LOVE.

CHAPTER 45

CASH IS KING. BUT LEGACY RULES

By Laura Parr

Success is relative. One person's success may mean very little to someone else, and there are 1000 ways to look at it. Yet if you ask people their definition of the word, it invariably falls into familiar categories – money, dream house, luxury car, notoriety, how you look, etc. We all fall into this trap at some point.

I did.

I previously ran my own property company for over a decade. I built it up to the point that when my first child arrived, I could step back, let someone else run things for me and take as much maternity as I wanted whilst maintaining my salary. I could see my little girl grow, and I enjoyed flexibility, income and time. Result.

You might think that this is my example of success. I'll admit, it is a great achievement that I'm very proud of!

But deep down, I hated it. When the time came for my manager to move on to other things, I had to decide to either grow the company or sell and start something new. The former option filled me with sheer dread.

I'd followed the money, and the passion for what I did was long gone. If ever there at all.

In fact, my biggest success is taking the leap to start all over again. I sold the property company and launched my coaching business. Now, I help women start and scale their own companies with solid foundations so they know it aligns with who they are. My speciality is combining the ability to create financial abundance whilst also using the business to give back socially or environmentally, creating a legacy and a dream life.

And I love it! I've already seen so much success, but still, with much growth. I work with incredible people, and, most importantly, it fires me up and fills me with so much joy being a part of so many incredible ventures that are ultimately making our planet a better place whilst also seeing my clients flourish! It fully aligns with who I am.

One of the best things about it is that I'm teaching my kids by example that values like fun, fulfilment, giving back & helping people or the environment is equally as important – if not more so – than prestige, money and materiality.

For me, success is being happy, knowing who you are, and living the absolute best life that you can – not the one limited by lacking beliefs or appeasing the expectations of others. It's a cliché, but success is about loving the journey and not seeing it as a destination where "you'll be happy when…." And ironically, things like money come far easier when you do this anyway!

So celebrate whatever successes you've had so far – there will be many if you look. And suppose you like the idea of building a business that provides freedom to live the life you want whilst also being a vehicle for leaving a lasting legacy. In that case, I'd love to chat. I thrive on this, and helping each other to achieve our successes only makes the journey – and the achievement – that much more satisfying.

Here's to your success, however, you define it.

CHAPTER 46

STRESS TO SUCCESS

By Laura Rowe

Removing negative stress from my life saved my life.

In 2017 I was given an 'all clear' result after a stage 2 Papillary Thyroid Carcinoma diagnosis, culminating from 34 years of chronic stress-related illnesses controlling my body and mind.

My adult life started with a bang. Abusive and controlling relationships, struggling to find my purpose, money worries, bereavement, expectations, deadlines, and weak friendships. Pressure around every corner I turned. It felt like I couldn't catch a break. Stress only became more chronic as the years went on.

I would swallow my feelings, building a shell of protection around my heart. Using avoidance tactics to distract myself, never dealing with my stresses.

Being in that heightened state of stress for years meant that my brain was catastrophising the slightest inconvenience and sending me into a deeper spin each time. I was trapped in a cycle.

Suffering from chronic migraines, covered in eczema, and constantly bloated. Over the years, I became allergic to almost everything (later diagnosed with Mast Cell Activation Syndrome MCAS).

I would flip between insomnia and sleep paralysis; my hair was falling out, my anxiety was through the roof, and my fatigue was next level. All of this only created more stress that my poor body and mind couldn't take, eventually being prescribed antidepressants and later diagnosed with Fibromyalgia.

Then the unthinkable happened… I received a Cancer diagnosis. Stage 2 Papillary Thyroid Carcinoma.

Enough was enough. Things needed to change, and fast.

Throughout my recovery, I would research my illness. In doing so, I discovered those illnesses had all been stress related. I learnt the powerful connection between the mind and body and how stress causes chemical changes in the body that create the perfect breeding ground for disease to grow. I was wearing my chronic stress all over my body for the world to see because I didn't acknowledge it, heal from it, and move through it.

So, I began the work on my emotional health with the goal of healing my physical health. Meditation, Yoga, journalling, talking kindly towards myself, a balanced diet, and lots of fresh air seemed too simple to work. But it did. I was dedicated to my practices, and in no time at all, things began to improve. My mindset was clearer, and my health was improving.

I quit my stressful, toxic job and began on a path of least resistance. Understanding my triggers and becoming mindfully connected with my thoughts and physical body. Soon I was teaching others to do the same globally. Creating fusion-style health classes that were not only holistic but scientifically proven to heal. My methods were not just working for others but having life-changing results for them too!

Don't get me wrong, I still get stressed; I'm human. But now, I am better equipped to deal with obstacles life throws at me in a more responsive and less reactive way.

And the best bit? I'm grateful for my cancer diagnosis. It was my pinnacle of change. It pivoted me from a path of distress to health and success. How can I not, in some way, be thankful for my life experiences and the powerful path of healing they have led me on?

CHAPTER 47

FLOURISHING WITH PROJECT ME

By Laura Toop

Life is full of uncertainty and things we can't control. There is no such thing as 'normal'.

The predictability of the 'linear life' is a myth learned at school. There are no 'neat' sequences it follows; indeed, change is the only constant in life. Yet, with change comes uncertainty and discomfort, a place no one likes sitting in at the best of times. Let alone when we didn't ask for it, hadn't expected it, or it reduces us to nothing. However, you see, the secret is that YOU are NOT nothing, and you can flourish with 'Project Me'.

School sets up the belief that if you follow the 'leader' (aka the teacher) and take the sequential steps, you will get your 'golden carrot', you place great attachment to achieving that 'golden carrot', and you dedicate much hard work and effort to achieving it. You define your success (or failure) based on achieving said golden carrot. Your identity is embroiled in it, so when you don't achieve the 'golden carrot' as fast or in the same way as others, you start comparing yourself, quickly your confidence is eroded as you continue to struggle to bridge the gap from here to there and to achieve your prize of 'success' - 'the golden carrot'....

So, if the education system has not taught you well, then what is the answer? Thrown into a world you hadn't expected, planned for, or worse still has gone altogether, what to do?

Following the 'leader' will only get you so far. Indeed, dealing with the emotional overwhelm and the stress of wondering how on earth you're going to bridge the gap from 'here' to 'there' can leave you numbing, denying, and avoiding your emotions just in the bid to deal with the 'gap' that has opened from 'here' to 'there', and that all illusive 'golden carrot'.

But it is in realising you're not nothing, and this is a very good place to start; life can keep coming at you, and you will continue to be grounded.

Symbols of achievement and success that signify you fit in and belong no longer matter because you already have success by belonging in your very own skin.

How do I know? Because following the spectacular implosion of my life in 2015, when I lost my husband, health, and career in a matter of weeks, I was reduced to nothing. Desperate not to return to the unhelpful coping mechanisms of the past (the eating disorders & associated addictions, the working harder & doing more) because none had worked, well, not long-term at any rate. I drew on the only thing I had left, myself and my ability to business plan. 'Project Me' was born on a beach, 5000 miles away. Today, I am living the reality of 'Project Me'. A calmer, stronger, more 'successful' me, and you can too, with your own 'Project Me', whatever the non-linear life has in store, still feel fulfilled and flourish, knowing you belong right where you are, in your very own skin.

CHAPTER 48

THE PAIN OF SUCCESS

By Leanne Hawker

Success is a funny thing. We often think about it only in terms of huge landmark moments, and we must remember to mark the smaller moments along the way.

When I was thinking about the successes I have had, for a moment, I couldn't think of anything I thought was worthy of writing about, and then it came to me. One of my biggest successes has been overcoming an illness, which inspired me to put my fingers on the keyboard!

When I was 28 years old and a single mother to a 5-year-old, I started to feel different, my body was aching, and some of my mobility was becoming more limited. It was little things at first, not being able to lift my shoulder up easily and a knee hurting when getting up and down, but over a few months, it started to get worse. I had no idea what was wrong with me. The pain increased to the point where I couldn't open a tin (have you ever cried over a tin of soup? I have!), I couldn't hold a knife and fork without being in immense pain, walking was difficult, I couldn't wash my own hair, and my daughter had to put my socks on. I had been working in a gym and enjoyed keeping fit, so finding myself in this position was difficult.

Turns out I had Rheumatoid Arthritis. I hadn't really heard of this before, and like many people thought arthritis was just something you got when you got older.

I was so upset, thinking that life as I knew it was over and I would never be able to do the things I could before.

Luckily, my GP was exceptional and arranged for me to be part of a medical trial programme which meant I got to see the rheumatology specialist sooner. I received my official diagnosis just before I turned 30 – what a gift, eh? – and given medication to help with the pain.

Life is very different now! I was always determined not to give up high heels, and I'm pleased to say I haven't; I am doing most things I did before, if not more! I've walked 100km to raise money for an arthritis charity, I am back teaching fitness, and for many years I voluntarily ran the local arthritis support group. It was so important to me to let other people know that a diagnosis didn't have to be the end.

What was the key to success? A determination to not be beaten. I wasn't ready to give up, and staying positive was important. It would have been so easy to curl up and lean into the negativity, but I wouldn't be where I am now if I had done that. Of course, everyone has varying levels of pain and mobility. Still, I believe a positive attitude and determination go a long way to successfully managing a long-term illness.

I sometimes forget that I have arthritis until I get hit by the extreme fatigue that can accompany it, but from where I was, that's doable! I'm so proud that I wasn't going to be beaten by it, which will always be a huge success.

CHAPTER 49

TAKE THE GIRL OUT OF CORPORATE

By Lesley Thomas

I had a typical upbringing. I was taught to work hard, do well at school, go to university, and get a job. And I did precisely this.

For 20 years, I worked in Corporate Telecommunications and made the most of every opportunity to explore the World. I had the joy of working in Dublin, Amsterdam, Zurich and Japan, staying in many of the best hotels and meeting many wonderful people.

Children came along. I didn't see the need to change anything, particularly as my husband had started his business, working from home. My mum-in-law had offered to come and look after the children in our house when they weren't in the nursery. We had the perfect setup.

However, I soon realised that having a job that required being in London frequently was not conducive to being a great mum, a great wife or a great employee. All the things I absolutely wanted to be.

So when an opportunity came for voluntary redundancy, I grabbed the chance to change my way of life and create a life by my design. I joined my husband in his business, where we sold ski property in Switzerland and added France to the portfolio.

To begin with, things were brilliant. No more clock watching, no more missing bedtime stories, no more boss to ask for time off. I was my own boss!

Working with my husband was fantastic. People joked that we were the Richard and Judy of the Property World. And most importantly, I was around for my children.

And then reality hit. Whilst I enjoyed working in our business, my role was functional. I loved supporting our clients, but the position was repetitive and did not match my natural strengths.

Honestly, the thought of doing the same thing every day horrified me. But what else could I do? I'd already been given a chance to change my life; was it greedy to expect another?

I had the same self-doubt that so many women experience. And allowing gratitude to hold me back. Thinking I must be grateful, who was I to want more. But the truth is I did want more.

I wanted to do something that fulfilled me. That stretched and pushed me outside my comfort zone; I wanted more.

As lockdown hit in 2020, I decided to retrain as a Business Coach. I had always coached and mentored informally and knew this was something I was good at and passionate about too.

Initially, I decided to be a Confidence Coach. But the more I studied, the more I saw the connection between confidence, self-worth, and self-value and how these significantly impact our relationship with money. This was my Eureka moment. The Money Confidence Academy and my 3rd Career was born.

This has been an incredible time for me. Probably the scariest of times. Taken out of my comfort zone regularly. With regular visits from the gifts that are Imposter Syndrome and Comparitinitus.

But I have never regretted my decision to believe in myself, to not settle for what I had and to back myself to create a life by my design. Has it been easy? No. Has it been worth it? Absolutely.

CHAPTER 50

SUCCESS – IT'S NOT ABOUT YOU!

By LeTysha Montgomery

My definition of success has changed in the past couple of years based on my personal experiences. I used to think you were successful if you were rich, famous and had a lot of money. Those are all status symbols that we see that make us think of success.

Being successful as an author is accolades, awards, book sales and being a best-selling author. With my first collaborative book, I became an Amazon #1 Best-Selling Author, which was a fantastic experience! Then it happened again with my third, fifth and eighth collaborative books. It's a tremendous feeling and a talking point if the seal is on your books at book signing events.

Next in my journey, along with being in more collaborative books, came more opportunities like being in various magazines, having my books sold in a bookstore in a national museum, doing an interview on local television and being on a billboard as a part of the books in two cities-Times Square (New York City) and Atlanta, Ga.

I've won some amazing awards like, Deborah Arise Marketplace Forerunner Award, Certificate of Achievement Global Impact Award and Presidential Lifetime Achievement Award. These are all once-in-a-lifetime achievements and accomplishments. Yes, they take hard work and dedication.

But you don't see all the years of grinding in my other business and sacrifice. So yes, it may seem like success has happened overnight in terms of being an author, but I have been a businesswoman for almost 17 years. I shared all those accomplishments with you not to brag but because that's what I thought success was as an author. Because that's what everyone seems to focus on. I am blessed with all those accomplishments and will probably have more, but that's not why I am an author. I am an author to educate and bring awareness about endometriosis which affects 1 in 10 women.

Let me tell you what success now means after being an author for almost three years and all the accomplishments. Success means that you share your story often and in as many places as possible, so other women don't suffer like you did. It means having a fellow author tell you that they read your story in volume one of a collaborative book, so they shared their story in volume two. It's receiving messages saying you researched more about endometriosis, helping so many women, or I enjoyed the book. Receiving the awards as well as nominations means that I am doing something right and being recognised for the work I am doing.

Ways to be successful:

Do what you love.

Don't focus on the success but on the impact on others.

Don't do it for the money.

Be true to yourself and don't change who you are.

Have a giving heart

Be open to new opportunities

CHAPTER 51

EVOLUTION OF THE SOUL

By Lisa Cattell

How often is success regarded as a series of painful experiences, with smatterings of positivity that may not even be joy?

Whilst this sounds bleak, the experiences I created throughout my life have undoubtedly fashioned transformations beyond anything remotely imaginable in my twenties. Could I have lived a life of joy and transmuted from this state?

Not when grown inside the masquerade of a Doomsday Cult, parading my many selves within deep insecurity, unworthiness and non-existence. Life appeared difficult beyond these young years, and the need for perfection yielded dramatic, suicidal outcomes (at worst), such as my miscarriage. I was too much to bear. But somehow able to summon help (from some unfathomable place) in the depths of despair and take positive steps ... the leap of faith needed to untangle threads inventing my mind's web.

From a fear-riddled, boundary-lacking, people-pleasing child with no idea of self to a calm, self-loving, compassionate being that remembers so much more of myself – the parts that have always been there, alongside the seemingly unsurmountable self-loathing, stubbornness and mischievous qualities.

Perhaps not always needing to be banished, but held in love and used in ways that support me, such as being stubborn enough not to have my first husband back (I have been getting through them).

Unravelling layers of my onion overcoat, peeling one after the other, to re-discover, all in perfect timing. These gifts are my true soul calling. Mini transformations birthing a truer version of myself, with increased personal power so strong now.

Meeting my soul needs more fully than ever with the pursuit of fun things long forgotten. Where did all the fun go – wrapped in the ever-consuming world of materialism and ego trappings with narcissist overlays. But I'm an empath – how can this be?

Wounds, what wounds? Am I not perfect just as I am. Perfectly imperfect each step of the way…why be perfect with nowhere further to explore. How will my soul be fully satisfied without excavating the patterns and emotions to return lost parts and feel more whole again?

Some of my deepest fears have been met through various methods of self-development and healing, including my shamanic work, allowing me to be freer than I have ever considered I could be: through self-forgiveness and increased love of myself, despite some of the despicable things I know I have done. I bet you want to know what they are, don't you?

Letting go of part of our sense of self is challenging, whether it serves us well. I mean, you don't know what not having something will feel like when you are used to feeling it, do you? Such as the ongoing inner critic tamed to a soft purr.

My soul knows exactly what it needs and how to get there. It always has. Questions asked helps my growth. Contrast is a stringent companion.

Bringing balance from an early split-off world, abounding in personal power and no longer hiding in as many unknown shadows masked by my ego as safety: unplugged voices, the echoes of others' paths, never my own that brought me to my knees continue to fall away – leading me inward on my journey to myself; a spine-tingling, head-spinning, future-making, soul evolution.

CHAPTER 52

LEAD WITH INNER FIRE

By Lisa Maria Cobble

In 2017, I started a new job, moving internally within an organisation, following an acquisition, and not liking the boss I inherited.

My new boss (replacement for the one I didn't like) was a breath of fresh air. I had been given an award and a chunk of money only a few months in as the programme I managed was recognised globally.

The job was easier than the one I left, and I really enjoyed working with the new people I met. Life was sweet.

So when a global initiative was launched on our site related to health and well-being, I was eager to get involved. It was the first time I had felt empowered to make my own decisions at work, and I leapt at the opportunity to join. I was a gym bunny, loved a good corporate challenge, had built/led teams in the battle for step counts, and felt it was a subject I could support.

I went to the intro meeting. It was everything I had hoped. The chance to put on events and programmes and bring new ideas and energy to the employees on our site towards their health/well-being. And they needed a leader....

I could not help myself….

I jumped at the opportunity. I had previously led teams on projects, events and business improvement initiatives. I was hugely passionate about this and could see vast opportunities. I was almost giddy with the ideas that had already flooded my head.

And so it was. I was the leader of a team of enthusiasts for our site; we served around 400 people in the factory and offices.

I was a little nervous about what my boss would say as this was a voluntary role, but, to my surprise, he THANKED me for my leadership! WOW! Pinch me!

And so began a two-year journey. We ran roadshows, courses, awareness sessions, and competitions, campaigned for better facilities, put on regular yoga and gym classes, got fruit delivered to the site and more.

The energy, passion and drive I had for the topic drew team members to volunteer their time and support. That energy, passion and drive was my INNER FIRE. It drove me to think about different angles, offerings and methods to deliver the programme. I used to joke that I loved doing it so much I could do it full time, then add, 'don't tell my boss!'.

After two years, a new opportunity appeared in leading a STEM outreach programme. And guess what?! I did it again! I had shifted roles to an engineering-based job, so it was only fitting I took on STEM too!

And with my INNER FIRE in my back pocket, I set to work with the same amount of zing. I led our site, then our campus (three sites), became a member of the UK Task Force, was nominated & won the STEM Learning Outstanding New STEM Ambassador Award 2020 for the UK and became part of the UK & Ireland Community Investment Board for the company.

I have learned to deploy my inner fire for things I am enthusiastic about - it delivers on many levels! I am happy to help others discover this via my coaching business.

Bring your INNER FIRE, and be happy x

CHAPTER 53

WHO KNEW STANDING UP FELT BRILLIANT?

By Lisa Simcox

Imagine a shy little girl sitting at the bottom of the stairs, eyes fixed on the bright white net curtains covering the front door.

Praying no one would turn up to collect me. I could still feel the warmth of the tears as they rolled down my face because I did not want to go to another friend's birthday party. But I was always forced to go because 'it was good for me'.

As I grew older, I realised it is ok to be quiet sometimes. And at other times, be described as bubbly and laughing loudly. But I did not always feel that confident.

Growing up, I wanted to be a hairdresser. At 16, I was summoned to the Head Mistress's office and was greeted by her stern-ness herself and my parents; this had to be the worst surprise party ever! Especially as I was given multiple reasons why my dream was not a great idea, so I remained at school. Although I like to think I would own multiple salons, have a major (and possibly global) brand and my own haircare range by now.

I stayed on like a good girl and went on to get a business degree which traditionally results in banking or accountancy. I know how thrilling that prospect is.

Who knew?

Turns out quite thrilling, as I got a job in London with a major bank on a management training programme.

Early on, I was asked to take on a critical business project which I took as a huge compliment.

Imagine walking into a room where the wooden panels on the walls were so dark, huge chandeliers were hanging from the ceiling, yet it was still gloomy. I could feel my hands shaking as it was scary walking into the project room, especially with a well-established group of experienced and seasoned professionals who were all men.

As I walked in, one of the gentlemen turned around and said, "I am so pleased to see you". Hoorah!! So far, so good. Until he finished the sentence with, "can you sort a coffee run before you sit down to take the meeting notes".

Picture this still fairly fresh into the business world; a young woman is faced with that situation. Part of me wanted to run away, another part to cry, and the best part was wanting to dig my heels in. Why had he done that? Because I was younger/female/who knows, he had judged me.

I took a breath and simply said, "good morning, everyone, my name is Lisa, and I am here to take over the management of this project" I sat down and started the meeting. That gentleman never apologised, but I learned a valuable lesson: always be confident in your abilities. And who knew standing up for yourself could feel so good, particularly when we successfully delivered.

I always remembered that lesson, and there were many other examples as I spent my corporate career in a male dominant industry.

Today I am a female entrepreneur with a successful small business where I wake up happy every day and get to do what I love to do. And I still stand up for myself and others as it feels good and is always the right thing to do.

CHAPTER 54

FINDING MY PURPOSE

By Liz Denton

Starting working life in a traditional career as a civil servant, I quickly realised I needed something more stretching than an administrative role. I wasn't sure what this yearning was, but I recognised that feeling as my intuition and ambition. It was my appetite for learning that opened new opportunities and I was soon promoted to management level, where I realised I had a natural gift for working with others, mentoring, coaching and training.

I was married and have two beautiful sons. I left the civil service and became a full-time Mum.

It was during these years that my mind became creatively messy. I had always envisioned a career, marriage, children, and the happy ever after. I hadn't expected this drive to do more, do something impactful, and make a difference. My creative projects became paid hobbies and a stressor rather than an outlet as I tried to convert them into something meaningful.

With both boys still in pre-school, I was diagnosed with Rheumatoid Arthritis shortly after with Sjogren's Disease and others. Demanding a massive change in my behaviour for me, physically and mentally. I had to adapt and accept it if we were to thrive.

My husband and I started our own photography business. Three years into the business, our eldest son was diagnosed with Type 1 Diabetes. Driving home from the hospital, I announced another massive change in direction. I needed to be present for our son 24/7, so I immediately gave up shooting weddings and commissions and so our photographic training company was born. We had always intended to develop a training arm for the business, and circumstances had simply nudged me into inspired action.

We worked all over the world, wrote articles and books and ran a myriad of workshops. We became very well respected in the industry and enjoyed the praise of our peers. However, behind closed doors, we were going through some very dark times. I found myself overwhelmed with anxiety and in a state of analysis paralysis. We divorced after 23 years of marriage.

Whilst coaching clients in the business of running a studio, marketing, sales, branding etc, their struggles with limiting beliefs like imposter syndrome, believing they're not good enough, were areas where I made the greatest impact with my clients, helping them realise their full potential. Opening their eyes to opportunities for growth and development. I love every minute of it. It lifts me up and gives me the joy to see their realisation.

Following divorce, I've been free to replenish and heal. I've had time to reflect on my journey and look for the learning. I've indulged my thirst for growth and worked with my wonderful mentor to qualify as an NLP Practitioner to give more to my clients and utilise those tools and techniques for my own well-being.

Looking back now, I see that all those hurdles I saw as struggles were gifts that brought me to this point of understanding my skills, feeling truly aligned with what was always my purpose: to empower others to realise their full potential. The secret sauce is to relish those struggles as they signal a new opportunity for growth.

Stop fighting it and embrace life. Stay flexible, explore and be inquisitive.

With Love, Liz x

CHAPTER 55

DITCH THE GUILT, GAIN YOUR FREEDOM

By Louisa Willcox

Being employed when you have children is exhausting. Constantly juggling work, children and home life. As a mother, we are expected to be 'expert' jugglers at everything in life. In reality, this is not the case and leads to burnout more often than not. We get lost, feel like we are failing, and eventually, the pressure gets too much.

I found this even harder being a SEN mum. My eldest son has Cerebral Palsy. Even though the work-life balance was widely advertised when I was employed, this was not the case. I don't believe there is enough education and understanding in offices about everything you need to be present for when raising a child with special needs.

I was constantly told I wasn't a team player, taking too much time off work, and then the opportunity to progress my career was stopped as I couldn't work full-time hours.

This should not be the case.

Sick of having to ask permission to take my own child to his hospital appointments, sick of feeling guilty that I was failing my employer or, worse, my own son, I decided to take a leap of faith.

I was made redundant and could not face going into another employed role. I did not want that kind of restriction.

I decided to set up my own Bookkeeping business, as I am a qualified bookkeeper. It started small initially, just enough to tide the month over, and then it boomed.

I now run my bookkeeping business, Best Kept Books and Consultancy Limited, and my Money Strategy business, which you can find on Facebook as 'Managing My Money,' where I help female entrepreneurs gain financial control and security; it's essential as an entrepreneur to know your numbers!

It has been challenging; there has been a lot of work, late nights and networking events. When you want to make a change, you have to work for it – but trust me, it is worth it in the end.

I have used and continue to use time-blocking techniques to manage my day, from waking up to bedtime. I work when my children are in bed, but being self-employed also allows me to take time off when I want. I can go for lunches with friends, spend time with my husband on his days off and still make money.

We need to lose the 9 to 5 belief and take control. There is another way, and you can have time and freedom.

Now, I can take my son to his appointments and be there for my children with no guilt or pressure. Dinners are prepared and cooked during the day, and I take time to look after my mental and physical health. Running my own businesses has given me complete control over my and my family's lives.

CHAPTER 56

YOU HAVE GREATNESS IN YOU!

By Magdalena Jameel

Never in my wildest dream did I think I would be sharing what success means to me? But here I am, writing this for someone who might think, "I achieved nothing, 0, zilch - so there is nothing to brag about. "... Wrong! I can say that because I was just like you and thinking the same... "What did I achieve in my life? ... nothing...." I'm here to remind you that you are worth it and to give you permission to celebrate your little (and bigger) wins too. As well as give you hope - more is coming because you are growing all the way to fulfil your dreams.

For many people, success means money. They relate success to financial achievement, and although there's nothing wrong with being rich, there are other perspectives on success. Many see themselves as a failure, not worthy, losers, not having achieved anything in life... (do you think that about yourself? STOP!!) People like me look up to these 6, 7, and even 8-figure earners and think success equals an abundance of money. There is nothing more depressing or false for most of us. I want to change your perception of success and open different horizons for you.

I came to the UK 18 years ago with my first husband and newborn baby. What I saw as a possibility for us to create a life for our family, my husband "saw" as an opportunity to be a teenager again with no responsibilities.

So, after I divorced him, I started living again. I remarried and have children in a mixed-faith relationship. I started a business from home, trying to build it with two toddlers, a husband working long hours and a teenager.

I tell you, it isn't easy, but I'm not someone who gives up. My home business has given me access to personal development, which helps me immensely with my mindset. My family are the people I hope one day will be proud of their mum and wife. Life has many challenges and requires me to work hard, but that work it's mostly on myself; everything else will fall nicely into place.

I also work full-time; I landed a role at a school (I never thought I would work in education, but here I am...). These are my achievements, and although I only have a chapter for you, I could write a book. A book about what many would think is failure after failure and nothing to show for it. And that's the point - I want you to know there is always something that you did great at, better than anything else, and better than most people. So be proud, achieve more, and have hope and hunger for more.

Wherever you are on your journey to fulfil your dreams, know you have raving fans and friends who are trying to open your eyes and say, "Look how far you have come! Look how much you achieved. You should be proud of yourself!" There are people like that in my life, who, time after time, remind me of this, so THANK YOU FROM THE BOTTOM OF MY HEART.

I'm that raving fan for you - GO ACHIEVE GREATNESS!

CHAPTER 57

THE LOVE OF SUCCESS

By Melitta Campbell

When I was asked to contribute a chapter to this book on success, my first thought was: "But am I successful enough?!"

Thankfully, I've been working on my mindset long enough to know that this is the fear behind all fears. It's a question that most of us ask ourselves before we embark on anything new. And I've learned that this is merely a question, not a fact. So, I challenged that thought: AM I successful enough? It leads me to the better question: What IS success?

To me, success is highly personal. What it looks and feels like can be very different for each of us. And there are times in my life when I had what looked like success but didn't have what felt like a success, and vice versa.

For example, I attracted many impressive and high-paying clients when I started my own business. When I talked about my work with others, their response told me I was successful. My bank balance told me I was successful. But inside, I was miserable. I wasn't engaging in work that felt meaningful.

The demands of my job kept me from being the present and happy Mum I wanted to be. However, I only realised this when I was eight years into my business and on the brink of burnout!

It was a really challenging moment. To realise that everything I'd been working so hard towards was taking me further and further from the life and impact I wanted.

At the same time, I remain grateful for that experience. Sometimes we must hit a brick wall or reach rock bottom. To have a clean slate, we need to think differently and create the experiences, relationships and life we want.

For me, hitting rock bottom woke me up to my situation. It showed me that I was focused on everyone else's definition of success, not my own. And it allowed me to choose to live and work differently. What a gift!

Since then, I've been on a more conscious journey to ensure that I am not just achieving what looks like success on the outside but what feels like success on the inside too.

Today, success for me feels much like love.

It's having quality time for the people I love and projects that light my soul. It's continuing to grow my skills and knowledge and helping others to grow alongside me. It's having the courage to say 'yes' to opportunities that both excite and scare me - and having the compassion and grace to not worry about the outcome. It's how, in noticing the little moments in every day that make me smile and feel alive, every day feels special.

The secret to success?

I don't believe there is one secret.

But if you create your own definition of success. Invest in yourself. Place boundaries around your own needs knowing this is self-full, not selfish. And keep learning, and you'll create the self-belief, energy and confidence needed to make even your biggest goals and dreams a reality.

CHAPTER 58

£30 AND A DREAM!

By Michelle Clarke

Almost 7 years ago, I began my own business from my couch after what can only be described as a face-palm moment and an epiphany.

My lifelong connection to crystals and all things spiritual could suddenly be the foundation of my future!!!

But the one person who should have been supportive wasn't.

Being a rebel at heart I ignored the demands to stop and soared ahead. I used half the weekly food budget to buy the first crystals and jumped straight in.

It was a huge mindset and skill shift from network marketing that I had been used to, but I was excited!

Within the first few hours, the initial stock had sold before it had even left the supplier's warehouse. I immediately bought more items using the profit I had made after paying back the food budget of £30.

My business started with a £30 loan, a dream and determination.

Each week business grew, and my stock expanded to overflow the small space I was working from. What a great problem to have.

It was not long before I added card readings, energy healing and spiritual coaching. I had created a tribe of like-minded women who, to this day, shout my name from the rooftops as the go-to woman for all things alignment, witchcraft and energetics.

Luckily, I had support and encouragement from those around me; family, friends and women I had never met. It's always baffled me how much of a deep soul connection we can make with people we have never met, but I wouldn't change it for the world!

These fantastic women have seen me and my business grow and transform. They have been part of my life for so long that they feel like family – what an absolute blessing!

Had I listened to that one person's opinions 7 years ago, I have no idea where I would be financially and mentally. I could have stopped before I even began, but I did not!

We all have wobbles, self-doubt creeping in, and the big and scary WHAT IF runs a thousand scenarios through your mind at lightning speed, and that's ok – how you react is the key to success. We get to choose our responses to whatever comes our way, and we are only responsible for our actions (or lack of).

Today, my business serves tens of thousands of women worldwide; I have been featured in multiple #1 bestsellers, blogs, and podcasts and was a featured columnist for a local magazine.

Little old me with her £30 and a dream!!!

PS You are not alone; I love you, you beautiful soul, and you are more than worthy and deserving of your dreams... WE ALL ARE!

CHAPTER 59

A WOMAN IN A MAN'S JOB

By Mila Johansen

Most people know me as a writing, publishing, and public speaking coach or as the teacher I have been for the past few centuries, oops, I mean decades. But in this chapter, I want to tell about a side of my life that will surprise you and that many people don't know about.

I often end up doing jobs that are meant for men. At one of my first jobs as a 19-year-old, I worked in the kitchen of a senior community. When the head dishwasher quit, I was promoted to the position. It turned out to be a leadership role, and I got to drive the delivery cart around, delivering meals to the various locations throughout the large complex.

Later, after college, when I married my husband, he put me to work on his organic citrus ranch. As the person, who did most of the housework and cooking from age twelve, he lucked out getting a "real Cinderella". We packed fruit 10 to 14 hours a day during harvest, which lasted anywhere from one month to three. Besides learning to conduct all the sales, I hired the crew, packed the fruit, and loaded it onto semis to be carried north to Oregon, Washington, and Canada. And I took care of the orchard the rest of the year.

When I started, the ranch didn't have a forklift, so we loaded every box by hand, lifting them up to be stacked on a wooden pallet. I always ensured I was in the line to stay strong.

I figure, between packing and loading, I lifted each of the 20,000 plus 25lb boxes twice. When we finally bought a forklift, guess who was expected to drive it and load the trucks with it—me. Sometimes we would have up to five semis waiting in a line on the road outside.

For the first few years, I worked beside my husband. He trained me in all aspects before he had to leave to work a day job to support the ranch. He left me in charge. At first, I worked alongside the workers, rotating into all the packing positions. But I soon realised that our sales were skyrocketing, and I needed to be on the phone. Lesson learned. My buyers all thanked me profusely for being more available, and our sales shot through the roof.

At one point, everything escalated to such a degree that I had to learn to delegate or die. I soon learned that the delegation's secret is finding the right person for each job. I have become a master delegator.

Another aspect was that I became famous in the fast-growing organic food industry, and men loved coming to ask my advice. I enjoyed this unexpected position of power and have now become a spokesperson for the organic industry. I also speak out against GMOs, pesticides, and insecticides.

My experience running a major citrus harvest has extended into all the leadership roles I have taken on since. I often compare it to going through a military boot camp. It turned out to be a fantastic training for life.

CHAPTER 60

THE JOURNEY OF MY SELF-DISCOVERY

By Mirela Buzila

Hi, my name is Mirela. I am from Romania, but I have lived in Bristol, UK, with my amazing family, since 2011. I love being by the sea, dancing and spending quality time with my loved ones.

I work as an interpreter; I am a Sales Leader with a beauty company and am also at the beginning of my property investment journey. I grew up in Romania surrounded by strong beliefs that impressing others is crucial, always looking for people's approval to go forward and with the mindset that women wash, clean, cook and look after the kids.

I came into the UK with borrowed money and lived in a shared house with my husband and my beautiful daughter Natalia for over 4 years. I joined a beauty company to keep me busy (as my daughter was only one-years-old at the time). After my daughter started nursery, I worked part-time in a cleaning company. In the meantime, I was trying hard to save money to have a deposit for buying a house. I was not appreciated, seen or heard at my job; I wanted more to bring light into people's lives, positively contribute to the planet, connect with people and touch other people's lives.

In the meantime, unfortunately, my husband got sick with cancer.

I was pregnant with my second baby, so I needed to keep going to get my family's needs met, as my husband was undergoing treatment. I felt trapped doing jobs that I hated. I felt alone and useless; my world was falling apart. Just before he got sick, we started the paperwork to get a mortgage towards a house with our saved money. The process was extremely slow, and my English at the time was not great, so I didn't know where we were, and I did not have the physical strength to deal with it. I prayed and supported my husband as much as possible whilst also looking after my daughter.

A few months passed, and we finally had good news that his treatment was finished; he was still following the checkups.

On the day he was discharged, we surprisingly received the key for our first-ever home and gave birth a month later to our beautiful son David.

A few months later, I started working again; I didn't know where to look or what else to do as I was so unhappy doing that job, but in the meantime, I couldn't afford to stay home. So, I started looking and listening to successful people's podcasts.

I realised it was about time to educate myself; I needed to know who I was and where I was going. I joined a course where I learned how to find my inner self and use my inner voice and instincts, and I wanted to learn more and more. It feels so good when you know who you are.

"To be yourself in a world constantly trying to make you something else is the greatest accomplishment." Ralph Waldo Emerson

The desire to be my own boss, follow my passion for helping others and spread positivity into the world pushed me to become an interpreter. I knew I had to fight for my dreams. I needed to achieve something every day toward my goals of being financially free, travelling the world and spending precious time with my family. That is how I got into the property investment journey (becoming a landlord). I successfully got rid of my implemented childhood beliefs.

You are unique. Love yourself. Love the life you live.

CHAPTER 61

DEEP HEALING JOURNEY

By Monika Mateja

I remember over 10 years ago when I saw my Mum again, after not seeing her for a while.

She was always keeping me safe and never wanted to bother me with any problems she had. My Mum was in the final stages of terminal cancer and signed off from any treatments into palliative care. I did not know how bad it was. Why?

I was living in a different country, and I was simply becoming a mum to my daughter, heavily pregnant I could not travel anywhere. These months were traumatic as I did not know how to enjoy my motherhood at the same time experiencing the quick progression of the illness and immense suffering of my beloved Mum.

Eventually, I did see her. I left my 3-month-old daughter and rushed to see her. And when I saw her, I wanted to burst into tears; she could not sit; she was half the size. She was in pain. I came back to the UK and knew I needed to take my daughter to say goodbye to her grandmother. I rushed to sort her passport, and a few weeks later, we were back in Poland. My Mum could not enjoy the hugs and playfulness with her granddaughter. She was too weak. I still remember leaving my daughter in a baby carrier by her bed so she could watch and talk to her a bit.

Something broke inside me. I always hid my emotions and sought a substitute to numb the pain or fill the void. The experience triggered massive emotions of guilt, regret, hopelessness, and unconditional love.

I could not understand everything that was happening to me at that time, until several years later. The seed was planted, but it was deep inside me, not wanting to come out.

That time taught me a lot and profoundly affected how I perceive my life today. Did I take any lessons from that experience at that time? Yes, I did, but I only understood them several years later when my Holistic Health business was born.

I truly believe that self-care is so important. Often, we have no mercy for our emotions, bodies constantly living in our heads, not in our hearts. To experience the true transformation is to go deep inside, heal the wounds, and take small steps towards the life you are meant to live.

My Mum died in a Hospice without me by her side. My daughter was born in May; she died in October of the same year. She left her journals describing her journey through the illness. Never able to tell that to anyone, she resorted to writing. They are heartbreaking to read, but I am glad I have them.

Her memory lives to this day, not only in our hearts but also our lives. I set up my business to create a legacy and to help others on their journey. I can't wait to talk about it with my grandchildren one day. Today I feel successful in being courageous to pursue my dream and, at the same time to live a beautiful holistic lifestyle with respect for my body and mind.

CHAPTER 62

INTERGENERATIONAL LIVING = SUCCESS!

By Naetha Uren

Intergenerational living can be a rewarding experience, but it is not without its challenges.

Six years ago, when our family was in a state of crisis, chaos and sadness, I would never have expected a successful outcome to the situation would be four generations (age 9-80) living under one roof.

Today success is intergenerational living.

Several years on, I have better understood and appreciated what it means to live together. I have experienced many joys and struggles while creating and managing a multi-generational home during Covid and starting a business.

In the beginning, all I had was hope and belief in the face of adversity that we could find a resolution to the current crisis.

I knew I had to continue moving forward even when I didn't know what the next move would be. Over the past five years, we have created our own unique way of life.

Our living arrangements would not work for all, it comes with its own set of distinctive challenges, but it also has many benefits. The first one that always comes to mind is my mom reading to her great-grandson every night; their relationship is priceless and a gentle reminder of why we do what we do on the hard days.

Our living arrangement has and continues to provide a sense of security, support, and companionship that benefits our whole family. There are, of course, practical things; it has helped reduce the financial burden of the cost of living, we were able to all be together during Covid, my mom is safe, and if she needs help or support, we are near enough to react quickly.

One of the key benefits of our intergenerational living is the strong family bonds we have built. My daughter has developed a close relationship with her grandmother; she sometimes says she has access to a human library book, where she learns from my mom's wisdom and lived experience. My grandson has a home surrounded by love and security; he has four adults who all want the best for him. My relationships with my daughter and grandson are deep, beautiful, and meaningful today.

We have all had to learn the importance of mutual respect, responsibility, understanding and compromise. It is not perfect, yet it is beautiful despite all its flaws. We still face many challenges; my husband and I struggle to maintain privacy, and my mom and daughter struggle to maintain independence. We all would like some more personal and private space, yet we have found a way to make this work.

Intergenerational living brings many highs and lows; however, it has been one of the most rewarding things I have done in my life.

Although I would not have defined this as success six years ago, today, it is.

Looking forward, would we change anything? Yes, our goal is to have one house with three front doors.

CHAPTER 63

I FIRED ALL MY CLIENTS

By Natalie Carthew

Last year, I fired all of my clients. Yes, you read that right – and no, I haven't lost my mind!

Everybody talks about scaling their business, but not me. I'm all about scaling back. For me, less is most definitely more.

Almost nine years ago, when my business was in its infancy, I left London for good. Relocating from the city to the countryside (Norfolk) was a decision that my husband and I quickly made one April evening. We realised we wanted to experience something totally different.

Our new life in the country began in a beautiful, detached five-bed house in a village set in just over a third of an acre. It was idyllic. Quiet but idyllic.

Fast forward to late 2020. We decided to leverage our mortgage-free status and invest in a cottage not far from where we were living. It was the culmination of a 10-year plan to have an asset that could give us a pension.

But then, in late 2021, I told my husband that I didn't want the next 30 years to look like my life did at that moment. I realised I was lonely. I needed life, I needed people, I needed noise. What I didn't need any more was more space than I could fill and the silence of the countryside.

So, we sold our house and moved into our teeny-tiny cottage. It was bliss. I was so happy, stepping outside my front door into a bustling market square, seeing, smelling, and hearing life all around me and experiencing the delight of hearing my son, Jack, on FaceTime when he was upstairs and I was downstairs.

We had totally downsized our lives. I gave away, sold, recycled and rehomed so many belongings. At that point, I realised I didn't need all this stuff. It was time to stop holding on to what wasn't serving my family or me.

Then I realised that it wasn't just my life that needed to be downsized – my business did too. I was helping my clients grow thriving businesses and generate great profits. But what I wasn't doing was serving me. It felt great to have grown my business from a husband-and-wife team to a team of four. But now that we are back to being a business of two, being in it for ourselves but not by ourselves, we're the happiest we've been in years.

For us, less is most certainly more.

Remember that it's your business. You get to decide what you want for it. So, walk to the beat of your own drum. I believe that trusting in yourself and your decisions will bring the greatest success of all – which means success on your terms.

So yes, I fired all my clients. And now, I choose to help female business owners build a sustainable sales process so they can connect with their ideal clients, have one irresistible offer, eliminate the feast or famine trap and enjoy a consistent income. That's what fires me up.

CHAPTER 64

WHEN THE UNIVERSE TELLS YOU, "SLOW DOWN"

By Nathalie Doremieux

How do you choose what is right for your family instead of what looks good on paper?

On the one hand, you have the voice that says, stay where you are; it's safe, it's what you know, and it's predictable. Are you really ready to give that up? And on the other hand, you have this deep feeling. I mean, in your gut, your body is telling you that this cannot continue forever?

In 1995, My husband and I were leaving the American dream: two French students fresh out of college and moving to the US on their own to go the dream and find a great job in Silicon Valley. Our families thought we were crazy, but we saw it as an adventure! And we made it!

We stayed in San Francisco for 10 years; we had three beautiful kids and a cabin in the mountains we would try to go to any weekend.

Everything looked great on paper, we were making a lot of money in biotech, and we had great friends from our ex-pat community. Until reality hit.

I will never forget the fear and the adrenaline rush through my veins when I hit the retainer wall on the side of the road.

I was at the wheel of our big 4-wheel drive Toyota Sequoia, my 5-year-old daughter in the backseat and I had just fallen asleep.

I somehow managed to prevent the car from going into a spin. Immediately looked at the back to see how my daughter was doing. I could see the fear and confusion in her eyes as the impact woke her up.

Guilt came rushing through my body, and I picked her up and held her in my arms, saying it was ok and that I was sorry.

Then there was that time when I fell asleep on the San Mateo bridge returning home, and bumped into the car in front of me.

That's two strikes and the Universe telling me to slow down.

So, when my husband asked if I wanted to move back to France, I said YES.

My husband had always wanted to be his own boss, so that was a perfect opportunity to start a new life, start a business, come back closer to family and build the lifestyle that we wanted for our family.

So, we did it. Sold the house, the cabin, and the three cars, moved our whole family (including two dogs and a cat) to a country our kids only knew as summer vacation with grandparents.

18 years later, I knew that this was the best decision ever.

We were able to choose where we wanted to live. We bought the house we wanted to live in, in the South of France, not too far from family (but not too close!).

I could take the kids to school and pick them up on time! (goodbye, late pickups and the guilt and shame that comes with it!). Our family now always comes first, and we figure out the rest.

Our business, The Membership Lab allows us to have the freedom to work from anywhere, with whoever we want, supporting other women like us who want to build a business on their terms.

CHAPTER 65

WHAT DOES IT MEAN TO BE A SUCCESSFUL WOMAN?

By Nicola Matthews

When I first heard about the subject of this book, it gave me real pause for thought.

Would I describe myself as successful? Probably not! And yet, to the outside world, I may appear to be. I was lucky to be born into a happy family with caring, supportive parents. I found school enjoyable – I enjoyed learning and never struggled academically. I always had plenty of friends. I met my husband at university, and we recently celebrated our 25-year anniversary. We have two happy, healthy children who bring us great joy. Life is good.

But is this success or just good fortune? Success, to me, implies a high level of effort. Some degree of sacrifice. Taking what you've been given and making the absolute best of it.

My business is the one aspect of my life that really ticks those boxes. Having worked in corporate roles since leaving university, I had never found the perfect fit for my career. I was always deemed capable and reliable but had never set the business world alight.

An international move in my late twenties gave me a change of scene and a different perspective, but at the end of our three years in the US, I was ready to come home and try something new again.

After a few more years back in the UK, we decided the time was right to start a family. And in a twist of fate, I was made redundant early in my pregnancy (completely unrelated as nobody knew I was pregnant at the time). So with no job to return to and a second baby on the way, I was out of the workplace for several years.

Once my youngest started preschool, my thoughts turned to the world of work. It had been a few years – did I still have relevant skills? How could we manage childcare? Would it end up costing more money than I could earn?

I began to consider self-employment as an option. I believed that the skills I had built up over the years were still valuable, and I started doing various training courses during preschool hours and once the kids were in bed. When I waved the youngest off to start school full-time, I felt more than ready to launch.

And now here I am, five years later and still in business. I have learnt to be selective about what I do and who I work with (unlike in the early days when I would grab anything that came my way).

Of course, there are days when everything seems to go wrong, and there are still the things I don't enjoy doing that need to be done, but overall, I love what I do.

So yes, I do feel successful when I think about my business. I can proudly look at what I've built and think, "I did that myself".

CHAPTER 66

PAY ATTENTION TO THE UNIVERSE "NUDGES"

By Nicky Price

As the alarm went off and my favourite radio station blurted out the usual cheery messages, I opened my eyes and had that same sinking feeling in the pit of my stomach that had become familiar over the past few weeks. The heavy sinking feelings felt overwhelming this morning, and I just wanted to hide from the world under the duvet.

But I couldn't.

So I just lay there momentarily and wondered if this was the lowest point in my life!

This all-encompassing grief from the loss of my best friend so soon after losing my Dad, coupled with my skin cancer diagnosis and a business that I no longer felt in alignment with, had started to fill me with anxiety that seemed to be taking over my life. Usually a bright and positive person - I was suddenly fearful of everything, I blamed myself, and now all I wanted to do was to hide.

Six months before...

To the outside world, I had a great life. A lovely home, great friends, an amazing family and a well-paid job in Corporate IT. I was even building an affiliate marketing business as my exit plan from Corporate life.

Life was good – and I had a lot to be grateful for, but I felt like something was missing. I felt disconnected from my "purpose" but didn't know what that was.

As soon as I gave up my job, I realised I didn't love my business ….and when your heart's not in something, the energy is all wrong. That's when it all went wrong, and I now call it my "crash and burn year" that resulted in my feelings that morning.

I believe that when you're not in alignment with the flow of life, the Universe gives you some nudges….and then an almighty shake-up!

Please don't wait for the shake-up – it's painful! Notice when something feels a little off because it indicates that you are drifting away from what's truly important to you at your core. You may feel out of alignment with something; you may feel, "is this it…." or you may feel disconnected.

So here's how to transform your life:

1. Understand that your life is a physical manifestation of the conversation that is going on in your head. Notice how you feel about yourself, what that inner dialogue is…and WHY. Go deep….get uncomfortable, and get help from a qualified Therapist to find what beliefs have been holding you back!

2. Get back in touch with your values and everything important to you.

3. Take small action steps that align with your values and needs, and tune back to your intuition to guide you.

4. Never give up – it's easy to stay average, but the path that is a little more tricky is SO worth it!

Seven years after my life fell to pieces – I now run a thriving Therapy & Coaching Practice running private and Online Therapy programs transforming the lives of my clients.

CHAPTER 67

UNLOCKING MY VOICE

By Nixie Foster

I am a storyteller, a weaver of words. I am the wild woman re-fleshing her bones. I am feminine divine. I am a mother. I answer the call of the wild and roar. Me, myself, and I!

But wait, I was not always this way.

There was a time when I was caged, afraid, shrunk down, small and unsure.

Like all good stories, let's begin at the beginning when outside I was small, but inside I had so much more. I was passionate and alive; I believed anything I wanted was possible. I was the dreamer, the creative one, with so much talent. And that was great, at primary school, when I was small. Not so much as I grew, and the cruel world began creeping in. What are you going to be? What and where are you going to study? I would tell them my dreams of writing and drawing, creating and performing; all to change the world into a better place. But no, I wasn't to do that; it wouldn't pay the bills. Defiantly I didn't do what I was meant to do. I was the campaigner, the vegetarian, the hippy-dippy crystal-bearing rock chick. I chose the subjects I wanted; art, theatre design and the token math because I was told, 'you can't study here without an academic subject'. Next came art school; wow, I had found a home. But the outside big was beginning to grow inside small. The big bad world was getting a hold.

Trauma!

This word I didn't understand. This word didn't live in my world…

At 16, I gave birth to a beautiful boy whose world was destroyed by mistake at birth. One that left him starved of oxygen and needing care, always.

By 21, I had done round after round of specialist appointments and attempts to find a way to help my boy, but a carer, not a mum I would be.

At 24, I entered a relationship that I now see as domestic violence but not at the time; for there were few bruises, no broken bones and little physical pain. There were words of shame, control of friends, no free will and token pocket money I gratefully received.

At 38, I broke; I lived in fear and could take no more.

No, trauma didn't live in my world.

At 39, I began to growl.

Then a light came on. I disentangled myself from the domestic violence situation. I rediscovered my love of crystals, the moon and my love of all things just a little bit woo. A few years passed, and the light began to shine, for I was to be a mum to a beautiful new life growing inside me.

As the world locked down, I sat with a small toddler and smiled; it was just you and me for a while. Then a while more. I found a community online that loosened the growl. I learnt and understood trauma. I unlocked the chains that held down the last part of my authentic self. I started creating my art again, began writing again, and published my children's story books. I stepped into my power of storyteller and roared. Now I empower women to unlock their voices too.

CHAPTER 68

BE STRONG TAKE COURAGE

By Olive Pellington

This is the story of what has become the cornerstone of who I am today. Back in high school, when there were already so many things going on externally and internally as a young woman, one incident was the birthplace of my confidence.

It happened during the leaver's assembly. We were the leavers and put on a huge show for the rest of the school to enjoy. My place had always been on the perimeter of a circle of friends, and they decided we would sing a song as part of the talent section of the show. It wasn't an easy song for a group of adolescent girls to pull off, but I did my part and practised in the shower for weeks.

By the day of the performance, there were only five girls on stage. We got into position, and the music started. To say I had stage fright was an understatement. There I was with the two leaders of the group and two others who were closer to the inner circle than I would ever be, in a room full of three hundred pairs of eyes, which wasn't including staff. I was so nervous my heart was struggling to beat, I could feel my blood freezing in my veins, and my legs felt like lead.

We took our cue and began to sing. My mouth opened, I could hear the song in my head, and I saw the video in my mind. I let them play. It helped take my mind away from the daunting reality of the stage. A few moments later, something caught me off, guard. From the corner of my eye, I could see the bottom of a shoe in mid-air.

I turned my head, mouth still moving, and realised the other girls had just run off stage, leaving me mid-verse. My instinct was to take off after them, but my mind was still playing the video, and the music was still loud in my ears. I wanted the trapdoor to swallow me whole. My whole world was collapsing around me.

This was it. It was decision time. I could either continue on the perimeter and forever be an unappreciated nobody, or I could break away. Instead of constantly looking in from the outside, I could be strong, take courage, be a true outsider and create my own path to success.

The decision was made just in time. I took a deep breath, closed my eyes and hit that strong, sliding high note that gave the whole song its true meaning.

When I opened my eyes, the crowd was cheering and whistling, and the teachers stood clapping. I did it! I made the decision, I bet on myself, and it worked out.

Remember, it's easy to do what everyone else does, but where does that get you? When you can be strong and take courage, you will get much further than you ever thought possible. There will be times when you fall, make mistakes and are fearful but do it anyway – that's what courage is. That's what keeps me going in business. So, no matter the circumstances, be strong and let your heart take courage (Psalms 27 verse 14).

CHAPTER 69

WHY NOT YOU TOO

By Olufunmi Olutile

It was just like yesterday when I decided to start my online business.

I had suffered a major setback of losing my family's fortune. I had decided to start a posh nursery and primary school, but 18 months later, we lost it all.

I was desperate to get us out of the hole, so I started researching. It wasn't long before I discovered the power of the internet.

At that time, I lived in Nigeria, Africa and often had a poor internet network. I relied majorly on generators when there was no power. I was too broke to get myself a fancy desktop or phone, so I would attend zoom meetings on my infinix phone which had a broken screen. I was just determined to find my space.

What happened next changed the trajectory of my entire story.

In my bid to position myself online, I struggled to learn the tech part. I had no choice but to figure things out alone because I couldn't afford to hire anyone, but I loved my discovery.

This was how I found my passion for building websites, funnels and automation. I further dialled into learning how to monetise this.

I first got a trickle of clients by offering free and cheap services. My geographical location didn't help much because of the stigma and stereotypes that, unfortunately, some ignorant people exhibited. It was hard, but I often remembered why. Oh, the power of why!

I poured back 80% of the sums I got paid into investing in my skills and personal development. I chose my mentors carefully and got certified as a business coach in business fundamentals. Slowly my hard work started to pay off. I began to be recognised for being attentive to my client's needs, creating beautiful websites and funnels that convert. I was taking them to the bank!

I, however, haven't stopped learning. Always a learner!

My big break came after disappointing comments from a client who found sending my charges through my payment gateway difficult. I then incorporated my company abroad, branded my business, raised my prices and launched my products and services. What happened next was phenomenal.

I stopped being in permanent hustle mode, started receiving invitations to speak on virtual stages, and began attracting clients who appreciated my work. Next, I was invited to be part of two anthologies which became amazon international bestsellers back to back. My confidence grew, and I finally started to feel successful.

I have since left my home country, and the life I lead today can only be attributed to God's grace.Three sentences I would leave with you…

Find your passion, sharpen your skills and keep learning.

Your past does not necessarily define your future, don't give it power over you.

Invest in mentoring and get to your destination faster.

If I can do it, why not you too!

CHAPTER 70

YES! YOU CAN CHANGE YOUR LIFE!

By Pamela Edwards

Are you living your best life?

Is your life congruent with your soul's purpose?

If you answered 'No' to those questions, then read on. I hope to inspire you to make changes to your life that will change your answers to 'YES!'

My life now is very different to the life I thought I would be living at the age I am now (69). However, this chapter is not just for those near or at retirement age; it is about inspiring you to explore & love life, to create a life in line with your purpose, whatever age you are!

When I was in my 20s, women were expected to get married, work until having a family, and maybe go back to work when the kids went to school in some dead-end part-time job. That's what I did, but the job became interesting and expanded over the years into a full-time career as an Office Manager/Company Secretary.

20 years ago, after over 25 years of marriage, I was destined to be retired with my husband and realised that I wasn't looking forward to what I saw in my future! I was definitely taken for granted, ignored, and certainly not appreciated. I wasn't prepared to accept it anymore!

I knew I needed to make changes. My kids were young men and didn't need Mum anymore. I decided to divorce & build a new life for myself, with no idea what that would look like!

I wasn't expecting that just a few years later, I was made redundant for the first time of what turned out to be five times in six years! I'd been working with my Brother for over 18 years – to say it was devastating is an understatement!

I was thrown into a deep depression but didn't realise it at the time as I was focused on keeping my head above water & getting another job after each redundancy!

I endured years of trying to find a great job while accumulating more debt and stress and seeing no way of escaping the depression that engulfed me.

I didn't know it then, but the Universe was trying to move me to where I am now. I was on the wrong path, but I wasn't listening.

I eventually started my own business working with people, helping them to create an exciting life and to step away from what doesn't work for them. I also work with Start Ups & Entrepreneurs to build and scale their businesses.

So many interesting stories to tell– there will have to be a bigger book!

My message is that you need to listen to the nudges from the Universe.

If you're uncomfortable where you are but still keep repeating the cycle, take a step back from your daily life and look at what the Universe is trying to do, then look at those questions again.

CHAPTER 71

SUCCEEDING CREATIVELY

By Paola Minekov

"You are so talented!"

"You just drew all this from your imagination!?!"

"I could never do that!"

As an artist, I hear this a lot. Art is often viewed as an inexplicable talent. You're either gifted or not. Yet, 'creative thinking' has become a catch-all term with little real meaning. As with everything else, thinking and succeeding creatively is a complex process. I'll share my secret recipe for success with you in this personal account.

My father, celebrated Bulgarian artist Ivan Minekov, a self-made man from humble beginnings, gave me one piece of advice when I turned eighteen. "Reach for the sky Paola, and you'll be amazed at how far you'll go."

Much has been said about visualisations, goals, and achievable targets. These concepts never gave me a simple explanation of why "Dream Big" actually works. You may only achieve some of your dreams. But aim high, and you will get much further than if you set yourself one of those realistic, achievable goals.

The Hive Mind - You don't have to go it alone. Don't limit your circle of contacts. This simple shift in attitude opened a world of adventures and opportunities for me. Furthermore, building relationships may require you to take the first steps. In networking, people call this 'follow-up'. Almost no one does it, but when you do, people welcome you into their circle, and magic happens.

Create your opportunities - The most important step I took as a professional artist was creating my own opportunities. For the first year or so after moving to London, I applied to various opportunities, got accepted to some and was rejected for others. To stand out, you must be the star of your own show. So, I began creating my own larger projects.

Consistency and the Creator's Block - Ideas, visual or otherwise, come easily to me. Nevertheless, I have also experienced the Creator's Block. In 1998 I needed to create a series of artworks for my graduation. I drew and drew. I started a canvas, painted over it and repeated the process. I got nowhere. Then one day, I took a cigarette break.

As I smoked, I drew a little painting concept on an A4. Then another. In the 10 minutes it took me to smoke that cigarette, I had six completed ideas. That day I created some of my best work to date.

I'd had a sudden burst of inspiration. How had that happened? Then it hit me; it was consistency, working day after day, regardless of the results. The very process of working had set the wheels of creative thinking in motion, and my seemingly unrelated ideas and associations had just come together. It's not about being gifted (though that helps). It is about training the mind and body.

Trust your gut - One of my biggest achievements is learning to trust my gut, no matter how outlandish the path it guided me on appeared. Once I started listening to my instincts and following my inner voice, I felt I had unlocked a hidden creative power. Importantly, I always regretted not trusting my intuition. If you have a hunch about something, follow it up. More often than not, you'll be proven right.

CHAPTER 72

CREATING A LIFE OF LOVE

By Patricia Heitz

What do you think is a successful woman? I find this a very subjective label. Through my journey as an Empowerment Coach and Health and Wellness Coach, I have found that every woman is successful in multiple areas and doesn't even realise it. One woman can be successful at being a Mom, ushering in the next generation of well-functioning, generous and educated adults to make amazing contributions to society. Another woman can be successful at business and finds a way to break the glass ceiling of stature and income. Most of us fall in between all the other labels we carry with all the duties we assign to ourselves.

My definition of success is learning to love myself unconditionally and utilising this state of being to emanate love and kindness to my family, friends and co-workers. This successful achievement took work. It doesn't come easy for anyone who works on this as a goal.

As women, we are taught that we are the caretakers; we are the behind-the-scenes, get things done without credit facilitators who are supposed to be happy with all our roles. We tolerate being treated unkindly and even abusively. We tolerate jobs we don't like, men we need to help us, and friends that do not contribute to our lives.

After surviving kidney cancer in 2002, I looked to make huge changes. I discovered what I had been through as a child, in an alcoholic, dysfunctional home, had created beliefs about myself that contributed greatly to my sense of not just lack of love for myself but, after answering essential questions about who I thought I was, actually hating who I was.

I know self-loathing contributed to my cancer, and I was determined to change that.

Fast forward to 2023, I am now a successful author, coach, mom, wife, friend and businesswoman. I could have never imagined I would become the person I am today; a person who gets up every day loving my life. I don't need to be upset at others because they are triggered by their own wounds…I understand now. I am now a person who can love unconditionally no matter what the behaviour or words because I unconditionally love myself. That is the operating system I now live with every day.

What is that operational system? LOVE.

Love is not just a word or a relationship. Love is an operational system that makes the world go around. It is an energy that permeates everything if we change the focus of how we see. Once I started loving myself and enjoying myself, I found everything I wanted to have/be just came to me. There was no struggle, no drama, no hoping and praying to be saved from whatever I had created in my life. I realised I had created exactly the life I had always wanted…one of love interspersed into everything in my life.

This is my success.

CHAPTER 73

THE GROWTH IN LONE WOLVES

By Penny Power OBE

There is a skill we can nurture and work on that is within all our capabilities. My words to you are about the subject of belonging, the impact this has and why it is essential for us all to emotionally bond and feel significant to others. This is undoubtedly one of the business skills that has helped me through many turbulent and painful periods in my life.

Maslow describes 'belonging' as one of our critical human needs. It is not new; it is as old as man, yet, we have lost this beautiful aspect of being human. Recently, a client I spoke to said, "when I started having deep connections, I started to heal".

A sense of belonging to a group, being part of a community, is central to our mental well-being and emotional stability. I have always believed that 'mental strength creates financial stability'.

For 30 years, I have dedicated myself to bringing this to the business world; sadly, we are all witnessing a rapid decline in our workplace, giving us the emotional support, we need. Shockingly, even when we are the owners of the business.

In a survey I conducted on LinkedIn in February 2023, 76% of people stated they were lone wolves.

We have all learned to be independent, to find inner drive, and to have self-survival skills, but how can companies and individuals grow and thrive when their staff are isolated and encouraged to self-rely.

We were created to be pack animals. Primal 'us' protected one another, knew our personal strengths, relied on and respected the strengths of others, and trusted others. In the pack, we didn't compete; we supported, hunted together, nurtured our 'community', and grew together.

There is no doubt with the growth of the Internet in the 1990s, we witnessed a place where we could all work remotely, the growth of competition, from businesses born from bedrooms to mass globalisation. We became lone wolves.

Technology has enabled connection, but only for productivity, marketing and shallow conversations; our worth is measured by the tasks we complete. Rarely do each of us feel we matter to others and feel safe in a world of constant change. We ask people to be vulnerable and real, yet what really encourages this level of trust and sense of safety.

Mental well-being is a challenge for us; we must look after our mental state the same way we manage our physical health. We need people around us, we need to feel worthy of the attention of others, to have ways to contribute and feel the contribution from others, and we need deep connections beyond the task in front of us. We must find time to listen, care and be part of something larger than our survival.

To wrap up, we have become familiar over the past 30 years with the concept of networking, a way to find people and transact. We are now in the age of 'community' when deeper connections and deeper needs are met. So as a leader, consider 'community'; as a citizen, find a community; it is the future.

In the age of Ai and mass automation, nothing else can differentiate us; creating belonging through community is the killer app until robots run the world. Let's hope we don't let go of our emotional needs and forget that we are human.

CHAPTER 74

SUCCESS BY DESIGN

By Philippa Scobie

"Sometimes, you have to be your own hero." This is the best piece of advice I've ever had, and it came from my wonderful, late and great father.

My dad was entrepreneurial himself and quite a character. While he always wanted the best for me, he wanted to ensure I knew how to get it out there. He would tell me to 'stop asking for stuff and go out there and do it.'

While he might have shattered my idealistic feminine sensibilities about knights in shining armour, he instilled in me a sense of independence that has only grown with age and experience as I've taken on different identities such as business owner, partner and the most important and rewarding of all…

…mother.

I've recently gone out there and 'got' a balanced, healthy approach to co-parenting. Firstly, I refuse to believe my children are from a 'broken' home. Society likes labels, but I don't.

I never have – especially since giving birth to a beautiful, loving boy whom society primarily sees as autistic. He will not be defined by that. Not on my watch.

So, I hate labels. They reduce people to one thing when we can be everything all at once. I've always seen beyond the surface-level stereotypes and found more meaningful identities underneath. For example, my broken family is now more loving and supportive than ever. We fixed it!

My husband and I made the mutual decision to divorce last year. Our second decision was how we would co-parent in a way that would lessen the emotional impact on our two boys.

If you've never heard of birdnesting or 'nesting', let me enlighten you as I was inspired when I read an article a few years back. Birdnesting is where the children stay in a property, whether it's the former family home or somewhere new. The parents live out of a suitcase, rotating who stays at the main house and when.

Always one for innovation and new approaches, I loved that my children's worlds would be as constant and consistent as possible rather than having to remember where their PE kit had been washed, and schoolbooks kept.

It has worked brilliantly for my two boys and helped them during a change. Of course, it hasn't been easy on them. Their parents have split, but the nesting process has made it a little easier.

As our first Christmas as a 'broken' family unit approached, my husband and I (and our new partners) agreed to spend it as one large unit in the home our boys were familiar with. How grown up was that? But again, it meant no mornings here and afternoons there. Having everything and everyone in one place was magical, and our boys were surrounded by love.

I appreciate not everyone's experience of divorce will be like this, but it is through periods of adversity that we get imaginative and inventive, whether it's business or personal.

Forget the labels. Forget how everyone else has done it before you. Your success is by design, and you're in complete control

CHAPTER 75

THE ABSENCE OF SUCCESS

By Phoenix Madley

I am relaxing in a crowded café, tuning in to the sound of coffee being brewed while gazing at my cup sitting on the table. The sensation of the porcelain in my hand and the aroma of the brown liquid fills my nostrils, warming my mouth and lips. The bottom of that cup is familiar. Success has been a pipe dream for me. Waiting for the cup to be filled. It seems like what is inside can only last as long as it is there. Success, sometimes we avoid it, like letting the coffee go cold. Other times we partake in it, worrying when it will run out. Yet soon enough, we will reach the bottom of that cup. Cold coffee on a hot day may seem pleasant, but we must adapt to our preferences.

I am unsuccessful in the conventional sense. The world demands the convental, nothing more than appearing to be doing well by having certain things. Yet it's possible to do well, to chase this elusive success by identifying it as being yourself. Life is ever-changing and moving, and everything is impermanent. We cannot take it for granted, yet often we do. We need to notice what we have. Having money, a career, good looks, and material things are what we envision. But some things still need to be put in our grasp, even when working towards our goals. The secret is to anchor success to its original position in life

There is a statement I use. One you might also find helpful. It is, "I am doing well." Despite how you feel or what is going on, this statement can create a space to acknowledge success.

Every time you breathe the air. When you wake up in the morning and can see shadows and light in your bedroom. When you get dressed and when you put your shoes on. Every time you eat something or drink a cup of tea or coffee, and every time, you feel emotions and reach out with happiness or sadness. Or when you connect with another person. Those things are a sign of success. You are okay as a person because you have accomplished being alive, which outshines any other thing you could ever accomplish. There is never a moment of unsuccessfulness.

We never have to see the cup as empty because it is full of the presence that you are giving it. The table upholds it and the floor upholds the table, and on it goes. Success is something you give to the world through your meaning. Objects and life phenomena only remind you of what was already inside of you. This is the mystery of experiencing success. That you are that image and not the world around you. The world can never take it away even when your cup appears empty or your circumstances come up trump. A sense of absence is really a sense of something being present. So then, there is only a presence and fullness of the absence of success or a presence and fullness of success. There is nowhere success is not.

CHAPTER 76

GOING FROM COLD TO SOLD

By Rachael Howourth

The secret code every entrepreneur wants to crack is HOW TO MAKE MORE SALES. Because selling is the lifeblood of business, and without it, we're just playing around and having fun.

Now don't get me wrong, I love having fun. But I wasn't having much of it when I was leading a corporate team with a £100million target to hit (*cold sweats)

And I didn't have that much fun when Covid destroyed my first business (a training consultancy).

But we move. Fast. I'm here to tell you, though, that you CAN have fun selling as a woman and make A LOT of money.

Hello, I'm Rachael Howourth, award-winning Global Sales & Business Mentor and Founder of Her Infinite Abundance. I'm going to share the secret of going from cold to sold so that you can create a life of freedom and abundance.

Selling = listening + problem solving

Selling doesn't mean you give off pushy used car salesman vibes.

Sales aren't about persuading. Or scripts, or the gift of the gab. It's about listening and matching your buyer's problem with your solution.

Think of it as a conversation between two people who can help each other. As long as your solution and their problem are aligned, buying from you becomes the next natural step.

A mindset of 'Selling is Serving' gives you a magnetic energy that everyone will buy into. Ask permission first!

One of the biggest sales secrets is permission-based sales, meaning you don't invite the sale unless the buyer gives you permission…. And that's half the work done!

For example, 'Now I've understood the result/outcome you want, I feel confident I can help you get there. I'd love to support you. What would you like to happen next?'

Give the power to the buyer; your role is the problem solver. It could be as simple as a DM on social media where you say, 'Would you like me to send the details for the offer?' You wait for them to say yes before you do it. They feel like they are in the driving seat and can make decisions. Much less ick, don't you think? Get comfortable saying "NO"

It sounds counterintuitive to turn down sales but trust me, sometimes it's necessary.

Your time is precious, so avoid doing sales calls with everyone and seek out your dreamiest clients. Screen all call requests and only invest your energy with perfectly aligned and 'ready to invest' leads. Your conversion rates should be 70% to 80%. Spending time with people still waiting to buy will lower your conversion rate, steal your time and result in less success.

In summary, your simple secrets to sales success are to shift your mindset from selling to serving, actively listen more than you talk, show you can solve their problem, ask powerful questions and invite them to give permission for you to share your offer with them, so they feel like they're in the driving seat.

When you master these steps, you can go from cold to sold with ease, not sleaze. And that's what we all want, right!

CHAPTER 77

CLEAR FEELING

By Rachel Bayford

"You'll be nothing without me", he screeched. "Nobody will want you; your second-hand goods now and just rubbish, dirty trash." He continued. "You're good for nothing, disgusting and thick." Putting me down, gaslighting and abusing me.

Words will stay with me forever. Not because I want to hang on to them for negative reasons, and I have tried all sorts to get those words out of my head in the past, but because now I use them to empower me, inspire me and push me forward. The best thing he ever did for me was to tell me I would be nothing. Thank you for the coal, I thought as I lit the fire. The fire within me.

Those dark nights spent alone crying on the en-suite floor were the loneliest. On many occasions, I thought about how to use the dressing gown cord to wrap around my neck and hang from the loft hatch. I looked at the box of paracetamol and contemplated ending it all.

However, I have always been a rebel, which was no different. I wouldn't put my dress on as a three-year-old because I wanted to wear dungarees, defiant in nature. I won't jump off a bridge; I will show him! I will prove that I am none of the above.

The bathroom floor was also where the soft inner voice came, prompting me to move forward and telling me there was light at the end of the tunnel. I could get up from the floor and move on from the abuse. It didn't come at first, and it was a while before I listened. But I suddenly remembered that my dad would say, "never let your belly know you've had a bad day", as a kid. I guess what he meant by that is, carry on. Get something to eat, and tomorrow is another day.

This is where the fight started, and the strength came. I had a 'lightbulb' moment, as I call it, where something just went off, and I knew at that moment that I would get past this. I wasn't any of the abusive things he called me, and his words were untrue. I just had a clear feeling.

I found things to be grateful for every day. If the traffic lights turned green as I approached and I didn't have to queue for ages, I would be grateful. If the person in front of me at the supermarket turned and smiled, I would be grateful. I would be grateful if the rain stopped in the afternoon and the sun started to come out. I began to realize that the more I was grateful, the more I had to be grateful for. Like attracts like. That's when the discovery of manifesting came, although I would call it asking the clouds back then. A life of gratitude. No cold tiled floors and a feeling deep within that defied all abuse.

CHAPTER 78

RE-CONNECTION IS MY SUCCESS

By Ramona Stronach

When I made the decision to leave my career to experience working for myself, I discovered something far greater than I could have imagined.

My life had been a steady path of what the outside world might consider successful; decent grades, university, vocational career, lovely places to live etc. Yet I felt like I needed to be more successful. I didn't feel free. I was always aware that 'there has to be something more' to life.

For too long, I had been looking for this 'sense of more' outside myself. In relationships, re-locations, changing work, in friends old and new and chasing exciting but fleeting experiences that I didn't know at the time were a distraction from facing myself.

After leaving my career, I could reflect on a deeper level about what I wanted beyond the desire to work for myself. I discovered that what I had been searching for was me.

My new path led me to learn about the incredible energy systems we are as humans and the subconscious mind's role in shaping our experiences and in the perfect time-space, the powerful energy tool of tapping - Emotional Freedom Technique - arrived into my life, and it began to support me in reconnecting to myself.

I learned that I wasn't my thoughts, beliefs or perceptions. I wasn't the painful emotions in my body. I began to learn how to relate to these emotions and to explore what was underneath them that needed to be released from my energy system.

I reconnected to my younger self, understanding her unmet needs and the perceptions she made that protected her as a child but have created big blocks in her adult life. It is she who holds the key to resolving unhelpful beliefs. And it is she who can help me change them.

And do you know what? I have found I have let go of chasing things outside of myself. That sense of 'there must be something more' has disappeared.

Opportunities have appeared that aligned with what I had imagined for myself because, energetically, I had moved into a place of receptivity. These experiences inspired me to found Tap Your Possible because so many of us are disconnected from ourselves – often without knowing it.

Reconnecting with myself has been my greatest personal success that has brought me more into alignment with the flow of life rather than in struggle with it. Of course, belief patterns will continue to come up and get the better of me. The undoing takes time. The difference is I can now hold space for them through awareness of their narratives and honouring my feelings. And the emotional charge around the patterns is released much more quickly.

If you are feeling less than successful in any area of your life, be compassionate with yourself. Take the time to acknowledge how you feel. Listen to those parts of you that feel disowned because they need to express themselves. Honour any emotional intensity you have because it is telling you something. Reassure yourself it is okay to feel whatever arises and that it is safe to let go of it.

When I connect to myself in this way, this is my success.

CHAPTER 79

AM I A FAILURE

By Rebecca Askew

I start my story from a negative place, a place where I didn't belong, a place I still feel needs a massive overhaul, secondary school. I was made to believe I would make nothing of my life, I was stupid, and I believed this.

Fast forward to July 2018, I am standing with my fellow students, waiting to collect my first-class honours degree in psychology. Does this sound like someone who was told not to bother to turn up for her maths exam because it was highly likely she would fail? By then, I was 50!!

The road was rocky; I suffered terribly from Imposter Syndrome, for most of the time I was studying for my degree, and juggled working and being a mum whilst studying. Throughout my studies, my dad's voice was always there, saying, 'if a job is worth doing, it's worth doing well, darling'. I live by this; the second rate has never been good enough for me; I am all in or all out.

When I knew my degree classification, everyone around me said it was what they expected, really? I thought I would barely scrape through!

I followed this with a Masters degree at one of the top universities in the world (a total waste of a year), but it taught me I could study and accomplish at an even higher level.

So, I now had the letters BSc and Ma after my name. What next? All my ideas before I started studying were no longer interesting to me.

And then, when my first grandchild came along, he didn't sleep (neither did any of my four children), but by now, I was a psychologist. I knew about sleep and the biological and psychological aspects of sleep. I knew the stock answer of 'some babies/children just don't sleep' was, in fact, incorrect. After a long internet search, I found a company that offered help, based in New Zealand of all places (we live in the UK). They worked wonders; I loved what they did, so I trained with them to become a sleep consultant.

I own a successful baby/child sleep training business and run my accredited training program. I absolutely love changing families' lives; sleep deprivation damages the whole family, not just the baby/child. Sleep has become my career and my passion. Did you know that you can survive longer without food than sleep?

So, what is success to me? It has always been about knowing I did my best, not to be the best, but to be the best version I could be. Stretching myself and not settling for just OK, being open to opportunities and creating opportunities.

So, what is my secret to success? It is NEVER to let anyone tell you, you need to be better or more capable. Always turn up and be the best version of yourself and never close your mind; you won't go far wrong.

CHAPTER 80

BREAKING THE SHACKLES

By Rikke Siegler

In September 2020, a harrowing incident happened at home, and I finally found the courage to break the shackles of my marriage.

For a decade, I had been married to a wolf in sheepskin. I was married to an abuser. Looking back, it looked like my happiness, joy, and energy were slowly but surely sucked out of me. My sense of reality and self were being manipulated. I constantly doubted myself. It was like I was a bystander in my own life.

The eye-opener was another serious incident that happened back in February 2018.

The police, the courts and social services became involved. I did not understand very much at the time. Trusted no one but my abuser. Strange but yet very normal. The dynamics of abuse is complicated and stretch over many levels.

To this day, the incident sowed the seed in my mind to realise something was wrong and not rosy.

Between 2018 and 2020, things on the emotional level grew worse. I became more and more isolated. Every day I prayed for a sign of when it was time to let go.

I was scared. Where could I go with no job, no money, no savings and five children, one with nonverbal autism and severe learning difficulties and another just starting the diagnosis process for the same issues?

I felt let down and betrayed by the system from the incident in 2018. Mistakes and errors did happen due to bureaucracy. However, the truth was because of the mind games, the violence and manipulation by my abuser and his enablers, I had, in fact, let myself down and betrayed my own true self.

It was tough. Not so much the fleeing in itself, even though we only got away with belongings which could fit into five big bags from Ikea. In my mind, I had already left. The hard part for me was actually accepting that the abuse had happened. I was in such a bad mental state that I did not grasp the extent of the abuse at the time.

Nearly two and half years on, it has not been all plain sailing or a walk in the park. The system is heavy when it comes to dealing with domestic abuse. There are still ongoing court battles and other unresolved issues.

It is a learning experience and a journey of personal growth. Some days are great. Other days could be better. I have learned to take a day at a time and realised it is okay to ask for help.

The success of my escape came when I started to trust the organisations and institutions involved with us. But most importantly, the magic to success comes from all the individuals and all the kind-hearted strangers I have met on my walk-in life since September 2020. They believed in me on days when I did not believe in myself.

Without them, there would not have been a successful escape. They will always and forever hold a special place in my heart.

CHAPTER 81

THE QUEEN OF PLAN B

By Rita Preston

Flying by the seat of my pants. Winging it. Going to Plan B. Throw me a curve, and I'll catch it! Sometimes Plans C, D, and E, thankful we have 26 letters in our alphabet. Yes, that's me: The Queen of Plan B!

I mulled several ideas in anticipation of the Successful Women book. I have been a good student, an average wife, an 'ok' stepmom, a cool grandma, a solid employee, a stellar volunteer (in my mind, at least), and hopefully, a decent friend and family member.

A former colleague asked me how I could transition from answering an intricate question to pleasantly answering the phone and then back to our discussion. My answer was, "because I am paid to smile on that phone."

Multi-tasking! Proud of myself; the more I could pile on, the better, from my day job to volunteering in the community. "Super Woman Syndrome", I have heard it called.

I thought that the more I did, the better person it made me. I was wrong. (I hate to be wrong).

It has taken decades, diagnosis of a chronic pain condition, normal ageing, global pandemic, and stark acceptance that life is temporary, to get me out of that mode. These things continue teaching me how to better use my improvisational skills.

I broke a hip. I hopped one-footed with my walker into volunteer meetings, chauffeured by my husband. No wonder some of my friends refer to my being 'crazy'! My improvising allowed me to easily overdo it.

I type this essay after recently accepting one more volunteer position, with another looming. To all appearances, I have not slowed down.

There is a difference this time: my acceptance was conditional on the board's understanding that I have a life beyond the organisation, that my family will come first, and that I am setting limits. The board voted to approve an assistant!

I need to improvise and provide alternative plans, not just for myself but for those with whom I live, work, and play.

It is unfair to them if I have not allowed them to learn the jobs (big or small) that I have tossed around my shoulders like a hero's cape.

I am no hero, nor do I need to wear a cape.

It is hard to let go, especially when there is a rampant lack of volunteerism in our society. Some of us were raised to help all that we can.

It is essential to learn that there are Plan B's available everywhere. There are others who can do our jobs, who will take up the sword when we can no longer battle. We must let others help, learning that Plan C may take a few steps back.

Improvising does not always mean finding a new way for myself to conquer a task, but rather it may be helping another talented person to find his/her path. The community will benefit, and so will I.

CHAPTER 82

I FOUND THE REAL ME

By Roberta Smart

Success is experienced on many levels, from reaching desired goals to winning over the competition. Still, often our greatest personal achievements are experienced deep within us, invisible to others. These are surely the most profound of all.

My greatest achievement, thus my greatest success, has been to learn to be Myself.

As a woman born to reluctant parents, I was raised to be a people pleaser, and I excelled in this so much that I completely lost my own identity.

I was, first and foremost, my mother's daughter; subsequently, I was a wife, a partner and a mother and I was profoundly Depressed throughout.

Amid all this, I became a Tarot Reader, a Psychic, a Healer and a Writer. I was proud to carry all enviable labels, but none were truly ME.

How many labels are you carrying right now that dictate the views of others and are, for the most part, worn for their benefit rather than your own?

Within each of us is a spark of the divine: our life force, our unique magic. I have spent years writing and therapy to find mine before stepping into a role as a guide and illuminator for others to help them find theirs.

My own spark is HUGE and BRILLIANT, yet for years, it was encased in a small quiet shell, hiding for fear of alerting attention and upsetting 'The Others'.

Discovering and connecting with her meant that I freed her from her prison cell and allowed her to move forward more and more until we became One Being, and I was home!

In 2019 I attended a workshop where we stated our dreams and aspirations. I dared to declare I wanted to create and perform a One Woman Show. (Having not stepped onto a stage for over 25 years!)

Shortly after, I happened upon a workshop teaching how to write a one-man show! Coincidence? I think not! Magic was afoot!

There I connected with a woman who was involved in the comedy scene in my hometown, who then took me to an Improv Comedy show. I joined the beginners' course learning Improv Techniques, and within three months, I was performing on stage to a sell-out audience of 180!

Stand-up comedy workshops followed, and I performed four stand-up routines and three Main Stage Shows in 2019.

I was up and running, thanks to my willingness to declare my Biggest Dream, notice the opportunities (and take them) and say YES to stepping out of the shadows and literally into the spotlight!

But my greatest success wasn't the performances, the skills I have learned, nor the delight of being with new friends I genuinely love but rather the rediscovery of my True Self beneath the mother struggling with depression, childhood trauma and the looming spectre of menopause as I turned 50!

Oh, and my kids are incredible humans who are changing the world, so there's that!

CHAPTER 83

INTUITION, FAITH AND TRUST

By Sarah Brigid Brown

"I expand in abundance, success and love every day as I inspire those around me to do the same."
Gay Hendricks

How about this for a positive affirmation?! I've borrowed this one from Gay Hendricks and his book, The Big Leap. Back in 2021, when I picked this book up again after listening to an inspiring online workshop for empaths, sensitives and intuitives (that's me!), here's what jumped out for me.

Whenever I reached higher levels of success, I often experienced personal dramas that clouded my world with unhappiness and prevented me from enjoying my success, like being betrayed by a friend, disowned by my mum or judged by my in-laws.

Oh my! This really, really hit home hard. I was finally able to see the repeating pattern for what it was. My fear of really stepping into and owning my success because it would cause me to end up all alone, be disloyal to my roots and leave people from my past behind. Or at least, that's what I thought. With this realisation came floods of memories of the times when I'd played down my success, whether that was winning an award for most promising solopreneur in France, becoming an international best-selling author or being mum to three bilingual, well-balanced and open-minded sons.

So, I started looking at all the successes I'd had to find the common denominator, to try and understand what had led me to feel successful in the first place. Each time, the notions of intuition, faith and trust were present, with a bit of going against the grain too!

These three notions cannot be found outside of me. Suppose I don't trust myself and have no faith in my choices, ideas and dreams. In that case, success will be hard to come by because I'll be relying on others to decide for me, comparing my ideas and living someone else's dream. That's what I experienced for many years, well into adulthood, until my consciousness shifted. I learnt to connect to the whisperings of my heart and soul, trust the intuitive nudges I was regularly getting, and define what success meant to me. And guess what? It wasn't what I thought it would be!

When I first started doing this, some people thought I was out of my mind, which I was, because I'd moved my consciousness out of my head and into my heart space. All of my successes have come after I followed the guidance from the Universe during meditation, journalling and/or oracle card reading. Learning to read the signs when a seemingly random email lands in my inbox, a friend invites me to join a group, or a post says the exact words I need to hear has expanded my life. This expansion makes me feel so whole inside, and that's how I inspire other people to find their way back to themselves because I feel the abundance, success and love every day.

An abundance of gratitude, success on all levels and love of life!

CHAPTER 84

NEVER TOO OLD TO SUCCEED

By Sarah Heron

My story begins in a dark place. Literally, physically and emotionally.

I've always struggled with my self-confidence, but work was where I found my confidence. As a primary school teacher, I was popular with parents and adored by the children. I worked hard at my craft, but it was a career that worked around my family. My husband was a teacher, and I got a job working in their little prep school when we had our two sons.

However, when my marriage broke down, my self-esteem was shattered. Around the same time, the school closed, making me redundant. After the disruption of the divorce, more upheaval. The boys changed schools, and I got a job at a local primary school. I threw myself into it and put their needs first. I had little choice, really, as I had no financial or otherwise support from my ex. Every Sunday morning, I was on the sidelines in all weather, watching the boys play rugby. I was the one marking my pupils' books while they played cricket. Their needs came first. Always.

I hid in big, baggy, black clothes, which reflected the dark place I was in. I wanted to be anonymous, and black was so easy to find. It became like a uniform in a way. Camouflage maybe.

More doom and gloom followed as work became very toxic, and after a nasty health scare, I hit a crossroads in my early 50s. With the encouragement of my new partner, I left teaching to pursue a dream. I'd always wanted to have my own business. It was an itch I'd wanted to scratch for years, and I knew the time was right.

I began my self-employed journey with a jewellery business. I was introduced to the world of colour and style through this business. I set up a collaboration with the world's largest colour consultancy company and was asked to present the collaboration at the company's annual conference, but I was asked to 'have my colours done' before giving the presentation.

As coloured drapes were placed in turn under my chin, across my shoulders, I could see instantly that some colours lit up my face, making me look really well. Younger even. Others made me look nauseous, highlighting the dark shadows under my eyes. I looked drained, like an old woman. Wow! What an amazing difference. I was blown away.

As soon as I began wearing my 'best' colours, the compliments flooded in, and my confidence skyrocketed. I knew then that I wanted to be able to offer other midlife women the same uplifting, transformational experience I'd had. I decided to retrain in colour analysis and launched my business' True Colours with Sarah Heron' during the first week of the first Covid-19 lockdown, and I absolutely love it! I have clients worldwide who love boosting the confidence of other women, matching them to the colours most in harmony with their natural colourings and suit them physiologically. It never feels like work!

From a dark start, I am now in a colourful, happy place with a successful business. I am a passionate believer that you're never too old, and it's never too late to do or be whatever you want to be!

CHAPTER 85

MY JOURNEY WITH OSTEOPEROSIS

By Sarah Mapes

My story begins with my grandmother. She came to live with my family after she became a widow. She loved babies and used to wait for my one-year-old son to wake up from his nap so she could hold and rock him back to sleep for an even longer nap. They had such precious time together!

My grandmother also loved travel and adventure. She enjoyed long walks and even ventured on roller coasters in her late eighties. She had such incredible spunk!

Everything in our life changed when she broke her hip with an osteoporotic fracture. She lost her mobility and freedom in one fell swoop. It was both devastating and heartbreaking. I became a full-time caregiver because she could not get around independently and had to use a wheelchair while she healed.

I helped her bathe, dress, and even go to the bathroom. These were all things she could previously do for herself, and we both felt frustrated and powerless. We followed the doctor's orders during the healing period, but there was very little guidance given to us after she had healed. We were never told that there were things she should avoid repeating a fracture or what she could do to strengthen her body after a fracture.

Years later, after my grandmother had passed away, I trained to become a yoga teacher. During my teacher training, one of my teachers, a physical therapist, mentioned that medical research had been done showing ways yoga could help with osteoporosis. I sat still in the crowded yoga room, stunned by the realisation that my grandmother could have done something to improve her bone health. This experience was life-changing for me.

After completing my yoga teacher training, I focused on learning how yoga and exercise can help improve bone health. I trained how to improve osteoporosis through specialised yoga and became a BoneFit certified fitness instructor. In my quest to understand what else could be done to help with osteoporosis, I engrossed myself in learning about nutrition and became a certified nutritional health coach through the Institute for Integrative Nutrition.

After years of preparation, I was ready to help others avoid the challenges grandmother and I had experienced years before. I started my own business to help women with bone density loss improve their bone health through bone strengthening and osteoporosis-safe yoga. I also coach how to cook and eat to maximise the nutrients needed for optimal bone health. It is incredibly rewarding to get up every day and work with fabulous women on their journey to reduce their risk of experiencing osteoporotic fractures.

If you or someone you know is struggling with bone density loss, check out my website at SarahMapes.co or The Bone Builder System channel on YouTube to learn about essential information for improving bone health.

CHAPTER 86

STEPS!!! RECOVERY!!! DOES IT WORK

By Satty Mann

I'm Satty, a grateful recovering alcoholic, compulsive gambler, addict, and adult child.

What an introduction!

My upbringing was unhappy. Externally my family were respected religiously and in the community. Behind closed doors, however, there was chaos, pain, and relentless physical and mental abuse. Aged 7, I climbed onto a stool, grabbed a bottle of aspirin, and swallowed the tiny round discs. I wanted to leave this disturbed world for half a century. Still here!

At 14, I dishonoured my family by breaking my silence. My betrayal saw me whisked to India and forced into an arranged marriage. My Father attempted to keep my mother and me in India, but soon we were back in Slough. That marriage was abusive! My father placed me with someone like himself.

When legally able, I left home thinking my life was my own, and no one would ever hurt me again. I was wrong. I worked and partied hard and took as many illegal substances as possible. This became my life for many years. I was promiscuous and didn't care about anyone.

Becoming a mum at 34, I felt inadequate for my little miracle. An angel from Social Services arrived and told me I could become what he needed. I was disabled and couldn't even lift him. Many outside agencies helped, and we are together because of their hard work.

My life was messy. I was drinking vodka upon waking. I needed substances to sleep. At the stroke of midnight, I became a gambler. I would gamble day and night and couldn't even feed my son. He went to school with duct tape around his shoes because I gambled the money. I put us both in danger for cash.

I hated life and the person I was, and I was going nowhere; LET ME DIE!!!!!!!

My first 12-step programme was my awakening aged 51. Five weeks later, I walked into my second 12-step programme. Trying to do it alone for four months led to two suicide attempts in December 2019. I HIT ROCK BOTTOM.

In the end, with nowhere to go, I looked inward and finally heard the message of Hope. Taking a risk, I reached out to someone to sponsor me, and she said yes! Our backgrounds were different, but she had this way about her. A gentle, calm, strong serene soul. Our journey was bumpy, but she had what I needed. With a combination of my Higher Power, the Big Book, external help with step four, her generous sponsorship and precious time, I was gifted a life. Over three years, I found sponsors in both programmes and worked on the steps in the other programme. I have learned how to be a woman, friend, and sister and, ultimately, to love the whole of me. No longer living in fear or isolation, I ask for help.

Proud and present as a mum, I make daily living amends to those I have hurt. The fear that held me in darkness and self-hate has gone. Today I choose to live in the light, love, and do the right thing. I CHOOSE LIFE.

I pay it forward today because of what I was given so freely.

Just for today, I will stay clean, sober and gamble-free.

CHAPTER 87

THE POWER OF SELF-BELIEF

By Sharon Brown

I had been brought up surrounded by positive thinking and self-help books. My Dad was an avid reader and what I would consider a total book-worm. He read three books at a time sometimes. I now believe that it was this constant exposure to those books, that has helped me live my life on purpose now.

My parents are both in their eighties now and in 2012 my Mum had a major health catastrophe. She was hours from death. However, death didn't take her thankfully and she made a full recovery. At that point, I was working in a Corporate job. I had 5 weeks holiday per year and it was a reasonably flexible place to work. However, I realised then that life can take a turn in an instant and if anything had happened to Mum at that point, I would only be allowed five days leave! I still find it insane that's all you get for an immediate family member.

I'm more than sure this was the moment I started to manifest my own future of self-employment and a laptop lifestyle, unbeknownst to me of course.

Fast forward a few years later and that position took an unexpected turn, forcing my hand to leave in order to hold on to my self-respect.

By that time I had started my own business on the side, an Events Agency. Gaining new employment, I jumped from the frying pan into the fire and began working for a company that placed zero value on its employees. My boss at that time had an alcohol issue and it showed, however it did allow me the time I needed to work on my business, so I didn't complain too much.

Eighteen months later… I jumped ship in probably one of the most rewarding ways an employee can… I'll keep that for anyone who wants to ask me how!

I was now self-employed officially and probably six months before I had planned for. Six months later in 2018 I started my first online membership group, namely, Revival Sanctuary. It came just when I needed it as I was feeling isolated and extremely lonely. I'd worked for 30 years straight in teams and suddenly I was on my own so the group of women who joined, were my saving grace at that time and still keep me relatively sane to this day!

Five years later and we're still going. The platform has evolved constantly and now we are simply a WhatsApp Group who meet up online and in person. Many of those original members are still with me and I have four online platforms to my name now (so far!). The community I built has followed me across platforms and taken part in the many opportunities offered.

I believe I manifested my ideal lifestyle through consistent thinking and envisioning it. I believe I can continue doing that and it will shape my life and my future. I live my laptop lifestyle and can work from anywhere in the world, which would have been a pipe dream 10 years ago.

If you want it…. think about it…. believe it can happen…. and it eventually will!

CHAPTER 88

WRITE FOR SUCCESS

By Sue Williams

Once again, I stared at the blank page in front of me. How long had I been struggling with writer's block? Perhaps, like me, you can relate to that frustrating feeling when your mind goes blank, and you just can't find the right words or any words! They've been locked away in a hidden room with no key.

Feeling lost and alone after the death of both my parents within a year of each other, I had also taken early retirement. This made me question who I was and what I wanted from life. I also suppressed my grief. People kept telling me to write, but I could not bring myself to.

After joining a women's networking group, I was inspired by listening to an uplifting talk. I decided to have some sessions with the speaker, a life coach. One day, that coach told me excitedly that she knew of a technique that she felt would help me... journaling in the morning.

At first, I felt deflated. Writing again!

However, the technique seemed straightforward. Get up half an hour earlier each morning and free write whatever thoughts, feelings, and experiences come to mind. And if I couldn't think of anything to write, I just kept writing that I could not think of anything to write. So, I committed.

To my surprise, ten days in, my words began to emerge in rhyme. It didn't mean much at first, but gradually I started writing verses and whole poems. The words flowed through me onto the page. I wrote numerous poems over the coming months.

Amazed at how my writing had transformed, I found I had enough poems to fill a book. I decided to self-publish and was delighted at what I had created. The book was a personal collection of my thoughts and feelings expressed through poetry. Not only that, but I used a colourful picture of my own face created by an artist on the cover.

As you can imagine, I love receiving positive feedback from people who have enjoyed my poetry, in particular, Believe, one of the earliest I wrote. The words of this poem have inspired me to publish three anthologies on the topic of self-belief for women and an oracle card deck. Both my poetry book and card deck app went on to win national awards. I was also honoured to recite "Believe" on stage in front of an audience of nearly 200 women. The room was so hushed you could have heard a pin drop!

Journaling in the morning changed my life more than I could have imagined. Not only helping me to overcome my writer's block, but it also led me to discover a new form of creative self-expression.

Overcoming resistance, such as I had with my writing, can lead to new discoveries and growth. Similarly, getting the proper support can help overcome grief and lead to success. Success the right way!

CHAPTER 89

FORTUNE FAVOURS THE BRAVE

By Susan Beesley

It's said, "FORTUNE FAVOURS THE BOLD, AND FORTUNE FAVOURS THE BRAVE."

That's my story growing up through school, my career and later the world of entrepreneurship.

At 67 years of age and looking back, I've got my Mum to thank for that because she encouraged that "NEVER TAKE NO FOR AN ANSWER" mindset which she'd had to adopt during her lifetime (I could write a book about her life and I will one day!)

So, where I am today, and the success I've achieved, is the lessons she taught me growing up.

Whenever someone said, "SUSAN, YOU CAN'T DO THAT" at school, she would say ", YES, YOU CAN". I wasn't the brightest of children, but I would always try my best to succeed… in fact, being told you can't just made me try harder – definitely a trait of successful women!

A child of the fifties (now one of the Boomer Generation), I was encouraged to go to school, get a good education and find a career until it was time to retire. I had other ideas when I had my first child and wanted to be what's known as a "STAY-AT-HOME MUM".

That was the start of my journey into entrepreneurship.

It was the year Prince William was born, and traditional baby clothes were all the rage. My Mum was a dressmaker by profession, and together we set up Classy Baby making hand-smocked baby clothes modelled on those worn by the young prince.

This was in the days before the internet, so we had to find innovative ways to market our business, ultimately finding ourselves featured in The Daily Telegraph through some brave moves! The orders flooded in, and Liberty of London asked us to make a range exclusively for them using their fabrics. I had my first taste of success and loved the buzz of working for myself.

Two years into the journey, my Dad died, and we sold the business as Mum couldn't carry on. I often think about what if that didn't happen, but life throws you curve balls, doesn't it?

What next?

I didn't want to return to working for someone else, so my next brainchild was born. With my career skills, I would provide secretarial services to local businesses. This expanded into providing bookkeeping services as I discovered that most needed to learn even if their business was profitable!

And then I met Chris, and life took on a new meaning. Aside from falling in love, he was also entrepreneurial, already running his own successful business, and helped me expand mine, taking my accountancy skills up a notch.

We've worked together ever since – an accountancy and management consultancy, a ski chalet business in France. In 2010 we gave up our traditional multiple six-figure businesses. We became online entrepreneurs with the aim of helping those in or approaching retirement achieve their lifestyle and financial goals… and we're still here doing what we love.

Words of Wisdom

Never take no for an answer - fortune definitely favours the brave. Never give up on your dreams of success because it's just around the corner. A woman cannot live on wine alone…

CHAPTER 90

KINDNESS IS FREE

By Susan Totman

Kind gestures, no matter how small, make people feel special. Just a quick word of appreciation or a smile goes a long way. This premise applies in business for me as well as personally.

Kindness can reap rewards for all parties in an interaction. The best part? There is no cost, monetarily or otherwise, that creates a constraint that would make it challenging to be kind. Yet people seem to have to work at it. I have always wondered why that is.

I was not always as generous with a good word or gesture as I am today. There have been points in my life during which I did not feel like smiling even when others tried to be kind to me. Despite that feeling at times, I have nearly always responded to that smile by flashing a quick smile. What you notice if you pay attention is that the other person's smile usually deepens and broadens when reciprocated. It took me many years to understand the correlation between accepting kindness and giving. There is a clear connection to wellbeing in sharing kindness. Some days a smile is all it takes to brighten an otherwise disastrous day for someone. I know – I have been on the receiving end of that kind smile at times.

Interestingly, applying kindness in my business relationships changed the way that I do business.

Working virtually can be difficult for many people and the shift to going online in business can cause significant anxiety and stress for some. Being cognizant of this is an important piece of understanding the business/client relationship. For example, extending empathy by understanding their reticence to give information freely – even necessary information - when someone new to the online experience comes aboard and patience when they ask 100 or more questions because they truly do not understand the process and sharing are small kindnesses that don't cost anything but a little time. Acknowledging and accommodating that different cultures work differently is huge and will garner respect.

To explain how the premise of kindness has affected me personally and in business is important to understand the context. Over the last few years, we have endured the heartbreaking tragedy of losing my little sister and then our grandson, both of whom passed tragically. During the aftermath of each of these crushing losses, my capability to work was decimated. We could not focus and could barely function. The very small kindnesses myself and my family have afforded personally and through our businesses became clear in an instant. The response from those around us was phenomenal, with hundreds of people citing that they were giving back to US. We weren't aware we had made that impact. The community surrounded us with love and kindness, taking care of us in our grief. We were shocked and humbled to think that what we perceived to be a few small contributions over the years had been observed and stored for future reference, to give back to us later. People from around the world reached out – people we had touched in one way or another without even realizing it.

Even the smallest kindness can change a life. Genuine kindness as an integral part of your life and business is powerful and will leave a lasting impression.

CHAPTER 91

FROM GRIEF TO GROWTH

By Tabby Kerwin

Life is hard… whether it is in business, as a parent, partner, friend or human, we are constantly tested, both physically and mentally.

One of the biggest tests we will likely experience at some point is grief. Very rarely, someone is a stranger to grief during their lifetime, whether that is the loss of a person, pet, job, lifestyle or opportunity. Grief surrounds us, and unless you embrace it and welcome it into your life, it can overwhelm and disrupt your life and health.

I am no stranger to grief… it has been a part of my life since childhood. My father died of cancer when I was 16 years old, and my brother died in 2014 after years of mental ill health. In 2018, my darling husband Simon died after a short illness of a Germ Cell Tumour.

Simon and I were not just life partners and parents but business partners too, so when he died, everything was fragile and had the potential to erupt around me. But I was determined to make everything we worked together on succeed and flourish.

I had previously experienced several years of depression and anxiety. My recovery was founded on strengthening my mindset and emotional fitness.

Still, Simon's death and navigating more grief would be the ultimate test of my resilience and emotional fitness. However, from the heartbreak and loss ultimately came flourishing and success... and my biggest success has been not just my own flourishing but my continued learning and sharing to help and support other people to perform and become emotionally fitter to protect their mental health.

Simon's influence and inspiration motivate me daily, and his death made me realise I was far stronger mentally than I had previously given myself credit for. This was down to consistent protective action to build my resilience and create my own happiness – no one will do that for you; it's our individual responsibility. I developed my own brand of positivity, not the toxic type where everything is going to be OK – it's not; life tests us constantly – but the meaning of positivity being I will be OK regardless of what happens, and based on my philosophy of The Three Ps: Possibility, Productivity and Performance, I believe we can all flourish and be resilient regardless of what is thrown at us. This mindset allows us to perform, and that's given me the strength to share my story through writing and speaking and working as an award-winning mindset coach.

Everything I do is founded on my three core values: kindness, freedom and growth. When you combine your values with doing the consistent daily work to be more resilient, emotionally fitter and more resilient, you start to succeed and feel real satisfaction in your life. You become the best version of yourself, and even when faced with the most difficult of situations, you can and will flourish too.

CHAPTER 92

THIS IS HOW I ROLL!!!

By Tabetha Burley

Anyone involved in my life has never seen the wheelchair first or viewed it as a roadblock, but Tabetha, as a person first, happens to use a wheelchair as a primary means of mobility and independence.

I am open-minded, positive, tenacious and vibrant, with a smile that lights up a room and always gets noticed. People often ask me how I remain so happy, driven and motivated.

Everything is a matter of perspective and what you choose to make it. Able-bodied people always view my inability to walk independently and having to roll versus walk as an unfortunate limitation. However, for me, I never knew what it was like to walk and lost the ability due to a tragic event; for me having all the abilities that able-bodied people view as "normal", whatever that really means anyway, I have nothing to compare it to. Therefore, anything I cannot do in the "normal" way is not a loss from my point of view.

I don't use the word …" can't."; instead, I say, "There is ALWAYS a way!"

I never would have been able to go to concerts, lead a life of active fitness, go skiing, or do hand-cycling with a negative mindset.

Without my confidence, I would not have been able to achieve the title of real estate broker among so many achievements throughout my life thus far.

If I had not initiated or tried anything for myself, there would have been many missed opportunities.

We, as a society, think inside the box far too often because the fear of rejection or failure does not even allow us to get started, and I would like to see that box blown wide open.

In my world, there has not been much I have not accomplished. Even if I adapted at times because I did not see a conformed path to follow or stay within the boundaries of a box, I see a road that keeps me rolling. Sure, I have had reservations and fears at times, as I am only human, but to allow those uncertainties to stop me would be more of a downfall; in my mind, that is just not an option.

It is a lifelong journey that sometimes needs help from someone who lives with daily challenges, someone who can show that having limitations does not mean a lack of motivation or achievement. The challenges can be an asset as we are forced to think ahead, think differently than the general population, and accept that not everyone can or will understand the struggles to gain true perspective. Believe it or not, people with any kind of challenge, be it visible or not, still have goals, dreams and aspirations.

To change the way society has been conditioned to believe that if anyone or anything is different than the prescribed definition of "normal" or a path you must follow, the idea or passion is not worth pursuing. People need to hear and see there are always ways to make anything go from a dream to reality, no matter what the circumstances or the limiting beliefs are in your mind. Our world has so much untapped potential due to these limits. How powerful is that? So what or who is really stopping you from reaching your full potential to pursue your passion and live your best life?

YOU !!

I would love to be the mentor / motivational speaker to FINALLY spearhead this much-needed and long-overdue change!

CHAPTER 93

WRITING EQUALS SUCCESS AND HAPPINESS

By Tracey Secker

Writing about my success has proven harder than I thought. I began by thinking about what success meant to me. I realised a lot of what I considered my success was around surviving and resilience, which isn't what the dictionary defines it as.

It uses words such as attainment, accomplishment, and aims - and some of my ideas for this piece fit with those.

My accomplishment of living with Duane's Syndrome and overcoming the bullying linked to it, surviving being a child victim of domestic abuse, getting up each day after a serious car accident and living through PTSD…..and others I have written about over time are all linked to resilience and surviving. But not the definition of success.

Then it struck me……' all the things I have written about over time.' And there it was. My success is my writing now.

So, my writing journey started at a young age.

Reading and my words didn't come easy, as my lack of confidence in my abilities began from an early age. But once I found them, I was hooked.

And this love of words and being able to retreat into my own world of fact, fiction and fantasy was fostered by a wonderful English teacher, Mrs Grant. She encouraged my creativity, gently showed me how to present words, and gave me some excellent feedback that made me want to write more and more.

I wanted to be a journalist as that was a way to continue my passion. I realised from experience that I needed a different path.

And then, various things in life came along to change my course to writing and put it on hold.

I did some writing over the years, business content and journals during a very challenging period. I attempted to bring back my words through courses, but nothing reignited what I felt while in Mrs Grant's classes.

I won't bore you with the details, but over the last few years, I have started to find myself. And one of the things about me is that I love writing. I am now a writer (of articles, blogs, marketing resources and content) and an author (my first solo book is due in 2023, and I have worked on two collaborations….so far). I'm passionate about words and conveying facts, ideas, thoughts and feelings.

And slowly, I am gaining some belief that I'm not a bad writer.

What would be my advice to you about success?

Whatever you are passionate about or want to do, never give up. Success doesn't have to be doing something to make money, gain status, or get other rewards. Success can be achieving things you didn't think were possible, but you go back to them just because they make you happy doing it.

And my writing makes me happy – the best success in the world!

CHAPTER 94

YES, I AM INSPIRATIONAL

By Trish Springsteen

We all have our own view and our own measurement of SUCCESS. For some, it is about business, money, and financial freedom; for others, it's about personal growth, educational achievements and awards. For many, it's about family and their children.

For a long time, for me, it was about my job – being good at my job. Then I developed my speaking skills, which was my first speech to an audience. Then when I started my business, it was all about the clients, their success and growing the business. Then I realised I could write, and with each book that followed, I acknowledged I was an author. Looking back, there is so much growth and success I can share.

However, the one thing that was the culmination of all those success stories was when I won a specific award, which I will share with you.

I had won a couple of awards a few years before this award, and I was so excited because they were third-party credibility for my growth as a mentor and as a business. This award was different – the nomination came out of the left field.

I have to admit when I received notification of the nomination, my first reaction was to dismiss it. This was not an award I could ever aspire to. Those were the negative, imposter syndrome thoughts going around in my head. We all have them at some time, and I can tell you they were really front and centre when I read the nomination and the details of the award.

One of my mantras in my business is I Believe in You Until YOU Believe in Yourself. This was the outcome of a lot of mindset work I did. Before all those success stories, I had no belief in myself, did not believe I had a message and had little confidence. I did well in my jobs, but I stayed in the background and dodged the spotlight.

My speaking skills gave me the confidence to step up, and as I grew, I started to believe in myself and what I was doing. I know the power of self-belief and how empowering that is to succeed in your life, career and business.

My other mantra is 60 seconds of insane courage – take 20 seconds to acknowledge the negative thoughts, 20 seconds to replace them with positive and 20 seconds to say yes, step up and grab opportunities.

So here I was, confident, absolutely believing in myself, ready to grab opportunities, suddenly faced with this award that had thrown me into a loop of negativity and self-doubt. It was an Inspirational Woman Award. I did not believe I was inspirational. I was good at what I did in my business, but I needed to be more inspirational.

I stopped, took a deep breath, remembered my 60 seconds of insane courage, and acknowledged that it was arrogant to not accept that someone thought I was inspirational. Who was I to say no to that nomination? I completed the nomination.

I was utterly shocked to win that award. It taught me to acknowledge that others see you differently than how you see yourself.

YES, I am inspirational! That award is my greatest success.

CHAPTER 95

SADNESS TO SUCCESS

By Valerie Clark

It all came to a head when I started having epileptic seizures; I was sent for a brain scan which, fortunately, revealed that I did not have anything sinister to worry about.

The Consultant informed me that trauma and stress can impact the brain, and he suggested these episodes had been brought on by stress, so we started to get curious and investigated what it could be.

I had not had a trauma as far as I was aware, the Consultant asked me a series of questions about my life as a child, and I completely crumbled during the appointment. He recommended that I get therapy. I immediately trawled the internet to find a plethora of information on exactly what I had experienced, called childhood trauma, a 'mother wound'.

"A mother wound is the pain, wounding and trauma carried by a mother and inherited by her children. It can be passed down 7 generations.

Often mothers like my mother, who have their own trauma wounds, don't realise the impact of their parenting or recognise they are emotionally absent, so they don't form an attachment to their child because they are busy protecting themselves.

Enough was enough, and I finally accepted that I needed to dig deep, so I signed up for an online Trauma Recovery Programme. This was life-changing for me.

It turned out I did have a childhood wound from my mother and an adult one from being married to a narcissist, which I had held in my mind and body my entire life.

I learnt that the mind and body hold onto trauma and that we can struggle with overwhelming anxiety and depression; we develop autoimmune diseases because of stress hormones released in our bodies, our brain tries to protect us, and our inner critics pop up to save us. All these things happened to me.

I felt empowered by this knowledge and decided to study Integrated trauma to help other women live the lives they deserve.

I studied hard, six days a week and qualified as an Integrated Trauma Coach, Positive Psychology & Wellbeing Coach, Cognitive Behaviour Therapist, Brainspotting Therapist and Advanced Narcissistic Specialist.

I changed my lifestyle, started Yoga and Qi Gong, which helped calm the mind monkeys, and read the meditation and positive psychology.

My passion now is to help women who are in midlife, menopausal, and struggling with the emotional mind.

Stress and anxiety can be caused by either a childhood or adult trauma such as childhood bullying, physical and emotional abuse, emotional eating, adult bullying in the home or workplace, self-sabotage, imposter syndrome, PTSD, addiction, midlife crisis or living with a narcissist and can show up, again, during the menopause.

Being successful does not always have to be financial; one of the biggest successes in my life is healing, finding out who I am and being the authentic me.

Healing is a journey, not a destination.

CHAPTER 96

COMPULSIVE GAMBLER TO MONEY MINDSET EXPERT

By Vivienne Joy

"Why are you putting money in there if you need it for food?" Said a curiously confused 7-year-old Vivienne.

I stood nervously beside the pretty bell fruit machine at the local bingo. I watched my mum getting angry and desperate, swearing at the machine for not paying her out. My Dad's hard-grafted 'building site Foreman' money clinking into the hopeless pit of misery. This became my familiar 'off school' afternoons and family time. I happily learnt to entertain myself by playing the old bingo tickets and eating crisps.

Sadly, this highly addictive, socially acceptable hobby created a lifetime of financial struggle and the reality of 'we just can't afford it' that SET MY BELIEF FOUNDATIONS FOR LIFE. On my 18th birthday, I celebrated with a day and night at bingo - happily legally allowed to gamble like the parents I looked up to. It felt normal. It was our everyday life.

Little did I know, I'd been thrust into a battle of compulsions, secret addictions, low self-worth, self-sabotage, overspending and fear-based work obsession; selling my soul for 15 hours a day to 'earn more to gamble' and pay the mortgage that at aged 19, I managed to get to stop my parents from losing the family home!

To the outside world, I looked ambitious and successful. My Dad's money map taught me to earn money and work hard like him. I felt truly loved, the three of us, a tight family. For many years, I described my childhood as perfect!

Aged 29, my parents passed within 8 months of each other. Gambling was a coping strategy, along with smoking, drinking, over-eating, recreational drugs and even habitual shopping! I tried to stop but always ended up back in front of the machines at bingo, arcades and casinos. My normal.

The real change came with a friend's NLP Foundation course. It was free, and I wanted to help and knew the life-changing power of experiencing it previously at work. The timeline process changed everything! My debt and self-sabotage were created by engrained normalised financial abuse. I was still abusing myself in the same way!

In the months that passed, I understood, accepted, released and reset my beliefs, and found new ways of feeling, being and behaving around money and other areas where low self-worth was showing up! As I transformed, I watched those around me change too! Others follow my lead to improve themselves… And so was born a new 'empowered' addiction. Helping people learn their worth and create a life of joy! I now train and certify Deep Structure NLP Coaches and help them build a business with sustainable income and impact to change the world.

I had the worst money mindset around earning, spending, investing, saving and self-care. I changed, you can too! Your upbringing has created your beliefs, feelings and behaviours - you live by them until, like me, you choose to change!

Think deeply; what did you learn about money and your value in the World, and is it true?

CHAPTER 97

A SPACE TO GRIEVE YOUR PET

By Wendy Andrew

My name is Wendy Andrew, and I live in Glasgow, Scotland, with my dog Pixie. I'm the founder of The Scottish Pet Bereavement Counselling Service and author of 'How to Recover from Pet Loss – Supporting You On Your Journey To Acceptance'.

As a professional dog walker, I am emotionally attached to the dogs in my care. I was extremely worried when I received a client's call informing me that their dog was very unwell and they were at the vet. I hoped I was saying the right things to support my client, who was understandably upset and distressed.

Thankfully, my client's dog pulled through and made a full recovery. But it got me thinking... I wondered if there was support for pet bereavement and immediately researched. I was inspired to do more.

In August 2019, I earned my Pet Bereavement Counselling qualification from The International School for Canine Psychology and Behaviour with distinction.

As I was conversing with people and sharing news of my achievement, many commented that they wished such a service had been available when their pet had crossed the rainbow bridge.

My original intention was to support my dog-walking clients when it came to saying goodbye, but it became apparent to me that this service should be available to anyone who needs it.

I studied various subjects, including meditation and journal therapy, to offer a holistic service and work through clients' grief together. Sadly, there is no cure for grief, so the best I can do is listen and equip them with tools which may ease their pain.

Many of my counselling clients have encountered 'Disenfranchised Grief' at this heart-breaking time. This is grief that is not acknowledged or supported in society. 'It's just a dog. Get another cat. Are you still going on about this? It's been X amount of time?' These unhelpful comments invalidated their experience and made them feel unsupported with nobody to talk to. They hadn't received the compassion that they needed, or it came with an expiry date. Disenfranchised grief is something I really want to challenge.

When the Pandemic hit, I moved the service completely online and began supporting people internationally. I also wrote my book, which was a #1 Hot New Release in 8 categories on Amazon when I self-published. I chose to self-publish because, for me, it was time critical. I was keen to offer a low-cost alternative to counselling when people suddenly lost all or part of their income and were isolated from their usual support networks of family, friends and co-workers.

Unfortunately, natural life cycles ended, and accidents still happened during this time of chaos which also caused many to surrender their pets to rescue shelters. I offer support to those who have suffered a forced separation for various reasons and volunteer with a group by co-hosting a monthly support group for victims of pet theft.

I have created a safe and judgement-free environment for people to talk about the loss of their beloved companion animals, regardless of species. A space where they feel acknowledged, supported and heard. I can advocate for them from the platform I have created, and I'm enormously proud of that.

CHAPTER 98

WHERE YOUR SUPERPOWERS LIE

By Yinka Ewuola

When I was younger, one of the things I was accused of the most was stubbornness.

It was said in many different ways… 'strong-willed', 'intractable', 'unyielding' – but it all came back to the same idea - that once my mind was made up, I wasn't changing it.

And as a little Nigerian girl growing up in a good Christian family, in some pretty hostile UK environments – that was about one of the worst things you could be accused of!

The adult world didn't want to have to deal with a stubborn child. The patriarchy definitely didn't want a stubborn female. The Church didn't want a stubborn…anyone, and you were rarely referred to as 'OMO DA DA' (or 'Good child', in Yoruba) – as 'stubborn' was not a welcomed feature.

It was a fail all round! The thing was… I wasn't TRYING to be stubborn; I just was.

I caught the upset and frustration of those in my environment early on. So, I set about working to be less stubborn. Be more flexible, and make my will 'less strong'. I would change so much of myself to please others and ensure I was more manageable. Palatable. Acceptable. So, each time that word would come back into my world… I would feel like I'd failed once again.

It got me down, as I'd see others easily give in to unfavourable positions for themselves and be rewarded with labels like 'selfless' and 'loving'. I did my best to follow suit. Until I discovered an insight that transformed my world in this and changed my life forever. Listening to an interview online, I discovered a powerful new truth…

"What you were told off for as a child, is where your natural superpowers lie.

They are the parts of you that showed natural excesses early on. You were 'too much in these things, without even trying. Because those around you cared about you and worried about how you would survive in a world that values conformity, because they didn't want you to receive the rejection or ire of the 'tribe' (for we humans are very much 'pack creatures'), they sought to curb those sides of you to make you more acceptable to the group and to keep you safe.

I cried when I heard those words.

I had spent years trying to move away from that part of me, to be less me and more of what they wanted me to be – and it had failed, and I was miserable. Because I was never meant to be less me…

"Safety is not the goal; survival is NOT the aim.

If you are to thrive in this world, leaning into those areas you were shunned and scolded for will see you make more progress and enjoy success beyond anything you've ever known".

Stubbornness wasn't the problem I had been told it was – it was a gift and it has been a gift that I have leaned into to create unrivalled success in several areas of my life, as I have channelled it into determination, resilience, consistency and grit.

So, think about your life and where you were told you were too much, as that's likely to be where your superpowers lie.

Then go be amazing. More. Never less.

Be chatty, bossy, quiet, bookish, emotional, opinionated, and stubborn……Be You!

CHAPTER 99

WHAT MATTERS MOST?

By Yvonne Hayes

I often pondered this, and with a background in education and training, it was my career goal to take people on a journey to develop their potential. However, there came a time when I wondered if I was achieving MY potential – was there more to life than the 9 to 5 with limited holidays? I thought the answer was to get more education, so I decided to get a Masters Degree. I DID get a better job but also longer hours and a frozen pension and salary! But now I was time-poor.

So, what was the answer – what mattered most to me?

Flexibility and an additional income.

At this time, I was fortunate enough to be offered the opportunity to work as an Independent Business Owner under the umbrella of an award-winning Global Company in the Health & Wellness sector.

Fab – I could see how this would give me the flexibility I was seeking, more time for my family and travel, and an unlimited earning potential.

But…could I do it? This was going to take me out of my comfort zone!

I soon realised that the Company had the most amazing training and support, which impressed me. I would be offered all the support I needed when I needed it.

The products were life-changing for me and continue to be natural, well-researched and award-winning.

I began by becoming an enthusiastic user of the products, happily and confidently recommending them to my friends and family.

An important step in my journey came during 'lockdown' when I realised I loved working from home and did not want to return to the office commute.

But I had to make changes for my 'side hustle' to replace my day job income.

I decided to put together a vision board and a goal map – outlining what matters most, why it matters, how I was going to get what I wanted and who would help me -as it is vital to surround yourself with positive people and a mentor.

I had an annual plan for what I needed to achieve, which I broke down into quarterly goals, monthly goals and a 7-day plan. I also have a 'day book' where I note my daily tasks, including working on my mindset.

I start the day with positive input from a podcast or a book chapter; I look at my Goal Map and check my diary (colour-coded for the different tasks), and then I have a Power Hour to work on my business. I often play my 'Power Playlist' to inspire my energy and focus.

Thanks to the progress I achieved in my business – I 'sacked the boss' in March 2022 and have not looked back!

I love being around positive, supportive people and making friends for life.

Leaving my Comfort Zone for the Adventure Zone (where the magic happens) has been the best decision I have ever made because it has supported and rewarded every step and has been fun.

Epilogue

We hope you enjoyed reading this book and have taken a lot from the lessons these ladies are sharing.

If you would like to be in the next book, get in touch with sharon@thebookchief.com

Everyone has a story to share and everyone can benefit from reading someone's story. Would you like someone to benefit from reading yours?

About the Creator

SHARON BROWN moved to the West Midlands in 2003 from Glasgow in Scotland. In 2006, as a sideline, Sharon started the first Speed-dating business in the West Midlands at the height of its popularity, which ran for two successful years. With a wide-ranging career in Event Management, Marketing, Project Management and board level support in various industries, Sharon started an Events Agency in 2015, now known as Lydian Group Ltd.

After realising that business was heading more towards the online digital space, Sharon left the Events Industry and launched four online platforms consecutively, the first being a Women in Business platform namely, Revival Sanctuary, in 2018 with a mission of creating an environment of 'Collaboration over Competition'.

Two further projects were launched during lockdown (2020) with the aim of helping small business owners build their brands through speaking, writing, publishing, and collaborative working. MO2VATE Magazine was created in six weeks from concept to implementation and received a fantastic following through its subscribers and supporters. It's now had a complete facelift as MO2VATE Media, seeing it evolve as a membership driven business and information hub.

The Speakers Index was the third platform to be launched as Sharon saw a gap in the market around Speaking Agencies and the lack of promotion towards their speakers. The Speakers Index is an online directory which also houses a quality Speakers Magazine highlighting the speakers' talents. Members are encouraged to create a full profile giving all the information needed by an Organiser who can then contact them directly through their contact details on the website or in the magazine.

The Book Chief Publishing House is Sharon's latest project, launched in 2021 and already with an impressive resume of clients and Authors. Sharon's vision was to provide an all-in-one affordable publishing service turning small business owners into credible authors through a robust and structured process. The Book Chief portfolio has exponentially grown during 2022 and continues to build huge momentum, onboarding clients mainly through referral marketing and retained Author portfolios.

SERVICES

MO2VATE MEDIA (formerly MO2VATE Magazine)

MO2VATE Media is a global digital business hub covering topics across business industries, health, inspiration, lifestyle, politics, opinion / research-based information, entrepreneur insights and many other topics, founded by Sharon Brown.

All articles are written by business owners and the project is managed by independent entrepreneurs. The online hub runs yearly International Awards and produces various books written by the Contributors who are part of the MO2VATE community.

Mo2vatemedia.com

editor@mo2vatemagazine.com

THE BOOK CHIEF PUBLISHING HOUSE

The Book Chief Publishing House was born during the latter end of the pandemic with a mission to support business owners and lovers of writing, on their path to becoming credible Authors.

The Book Chief publishes every age group, genre, type and size of book and advises on every step of producing Authors books from book covers, titles, book descriptions, and growing through the relevant rankings on Amazon and much more.

The Book Chief has a great track record in customer service and of producing great results for Authors books, in layout, editing, design and marketing.

As a one-stop shop for all Publishing needs, and payment plans to spread the cost, it should be the first stop for those looking to publish and spread the word about their book! Lots of additional services to choose from too!

Thebookchief.com

sharon@thebookchief.com

THE SPEAKERS INDEX

The Speakers Index is an online directory for speakers and event organisers designed to improve their chances of being seen by the right people.

We produce a quarterly magazine where each speaker features on a double page spread. The magazine is sent out through social media and to our email list on each publication.

Working similar to an agency but without any additional fees or commission, The Speakers Index also creates events to allow speakers to participate and be seen.

Thespeakersindex.com
sharon@thespeakersindex.com

REVIVAL SANCTUARY

Revival Sanctuary was the very first online platform founded by Sharon Brown in 2018, designed to create an environment of support, encouragement and celebration for women in business. With a mission to help women embrace a mindset of collaboration over competition, Revival created a beautiful safe space for women who join, to be completely themselves, without judgement.

The platform comprises a WhatsApp group for real time conversation and discussion. Quarterly meet-ups are organised in London with varying activities for the ladies to join in and just enjoy a great day connecting and having fun and online coffee chats happen monthly to allow overseas members to connect with anyone who joins in.

sharon@revivalsanctuary.co.uk

Printed in Great Britain
by Amazon

33102333R00126